A Principal's Guide

Guide

to Special Education

Third Edition

David F. Bateman and C. Fred Bateman

Council for
Exceptional
Children
The voice and vision of special education

Council for Exceptional Children
2900 Crystal Drive, Suite 1000
Arlington, VA 22202
www.cec.sped.org

Library of Congress Cataloging-in-Publication data

Bateman, David F.
    A principal's guide to special education / by David F. Bateman and C. Fred Bateman.
    p. cm.
    Includes biographical references.

ISBN 978-0-86586-479-5 (soft cover edition)
ISBN 978-0-86586-489-4 (eBook edition)

Cover and interior design by Tom Karabatakis.

Printed in the United States of America by Sheridan Books, Inc.
Third edition

10 9 8 7 6 5

Contents

Acknowledgments

In developing the third edition of *A Principal's Guide to Special Education*, we received valuable input from the National Association of Secondary School Principals (NASSP) and the National Association of Elementary School Principals (NAESP). These organizations were able to highlight for us the particular concerns of their members as well as validate the topics we had identified through our continuing work and interviews with teachers and administrators as being essential to the third edition. In particular, we appreciate the early advice from Chris Mason (formerly of NAESP) and the continuing enthusiastic support of John Nori (NASSP) and Martha Morris (NAESP).

The Council for Exceptional Children (CEC) has, since the first edition of this book, supported our goals for ensuring that administrators in both elementary and secondary settings have access to the resources they need to effectively serve the needs of students with disabilities. Luann Purcell, of the Council of Administrators of Special Education (CASE), a CEC division, has supported our efforts to facilitate communication between principals and other administrators. We would also like to thank the production staff at CEC who have repeatedly shown the advantages of working with professional editors and the enormous benefits they provide, especially Lorraine Sobson. She and her staff were a great help to us in polishing this most recent edition.

We were also greatly assisted by others in the field with knowledge of and experience in the topics this edition addresses. Chapter 2 relies heavily on the work of Ron Miros, who assisted us with the first and second editions of the book, as well. His support is greatly appreciated and we are indebted to him.

In addition, our thanks go to the following individuals for their input and assistance: Corinne Eisenhart, Shippensburg University (Chapter 6); Calli Lewis, California State University-Bakersfield, Kelly Carrero, Shippensburg University, and Mandy Lusk, Clayton State University (Chapter 7); Christopher Schwilk, Shippensburg University (Chapter 8); Todd Whitman, Shippensburg University, and Mark Ryan, (Chapter 9); and Elizabeth Alves, South Middleton School District, and Heather Hess, Ridgway Area School District (Chapter 10).

Futher, we would like to thank the following individuals who were instrumental in the development of earlier editions of *A Principal's Guide*: Jan Andrejco, Alan Vaughan, Kevin Koury, Katherine Mithchum, Johanna Tesman, Susan Foltz, Dorothy O'Shea, and Lawrence O'Shea.

Introduction

This is a book for school principals. We are well aware of the complexities that you face in your jobs. In many ways you are the focal point of today's discussions about public education: You are judged on the achievement of your students, the quality of your teachers, the level of decorum in your building, the dropout rate of your students, and even the success of your athletic teams.

To handle the close scrutiny of reporters, families, local politicians, and central office bosses, principals need to have effective management techniques, extraordinary patience, and strong problem-solving skills. In addition, you must be familiar with the various subjects that are taught in your school, and must keep abreast of the latest research regarding the best ways to measure student progress and teacher effectiveness. You must be ready to speak—without sounding defensive—when an incident occurs in or around the school, and what you plan to do about it, all the while evaluating whether or not the superintendent needs to know everything (or just the things that might show up on the six o'clock news).

One thread that runs throughout all these issues is how to provide special education services to children who come to school with learning, mental, social and emotional, or physical disabilities. Both teachers and parents will naturally look to you, as the leader of the school, to guide them in their meetings regarding these matters. Yet, it is doubtful that you have had the time to keep up with the ever-changing laws and regulations—to say nothing about the volumes of court decisions—that guide providing special education services.

This book was prepared for you with all of that in mind and is based on the type of problems principals face daily, and the type of questions they have asked us regarding these matters. We have pulled together a guide specifically for you, to help steer you through the maze of issues that you may face as you coordinate the daily work in your school, especially with regards to the education of children with disabilities.

As you will see, this guide encompasses a wide variety of topics, from the basic legal framework to issues regarding staffing, curriculum, student education plans, placement decisions, classroom management, assessment, and discipline. We have organized this guide so that you can use it as a reference for whatever type of situation you encounter. The appendices provide tools to help you manage your special education services and informational resources in the event that you need to dig a little deeper into any of the topics discussed.

A Principal's Primary Responsibilities

This book is organized around nine very important themes:

1. The principal is responsible for the education of all students in the school.
2. The principal needs to be familiar with the concept and practice of special education.
3. The principal needs to ensure that staff members know what is necessary for providing special education services.
4. The principal needs to verify that staff members are appropriately implementing services for students with disabilities.
5. The principal should lead efforts for data collection.
6. The principal should ensure that all staff members are aware of the process for identifying students with disabilities.
7. The principal must be prepared to lead meetings related to services for students with disabilities.
8. The principal needs to know all students in the building and be ready to talk about them.
9. The principal needs to know how to prevent discipline problems.

These themes underlie our concept of the principal as instructional leader, and they are integrated into every chapter of this guide.

The Principal Is Responsible for the Education of All Students in the School

From the first day children are assigned to a school, their education becomes the responsibility of the principal. Many parents of students with disabilities may not know the special education director for their school district, but they know the name of and how to contact the principal at their child's school. Along with being this point of contact for parents comes the responsibility of making sure all students in the school receive an appropriate education. With this expectation, the principal needs to make sure staff include adequately trained special education teachers and related services personnel, and that the education team meets the specific timelines and requirements for providing special education services. The principal needs to be able to explain to all—staff, families, and outside evaluators—the procedures used to comply with special education regulations. This is a very important part of the process.

The Principal Needs to Be Familiar With the Concept and Practice of Special Education

Most principals are not trained in special education. However, the principal needs to know about special education services and the different types of special education staff. Principals should be prepared to participate in special education evaluation meetings, individualized education program (IEP) meetings, and discipline meetings, and should periodically observe special education classroom instruction—just like they observe general education classroom instruction. Appendix A provides some helpful Internet resources to enhance your understanding of special education topics.

The Principal Needs to Ensure That Staff Members Know What Is Necessary for Providing Special Education Services

For families, each school representative is a very important part of their child's education. For some parents, the main point of contact is the only school employee they see, the school bus driver. Because families see every school representative as a very important part of their child's education, every staff member in the school must understand the need to look out for children with disabilities and report to others when they see problems. It is also vitally important that principals train staff so that children with disabilities are included—not only for academic instruction, but also in the extracurricular components of a school. A principal should continually communicate with staff to make sure these students' needs are being met and that they know their responsibilities towards students with disabilities—and ensure that all staff members are carrying out those responsibilities.

The Principal Needs to Verify That Staff Members Are Appropriately Implementing Services for Students With Disabilities

Even if your district is lucky enough to have a hands-on special education director who is in your building frequently monitoring services, that director is responsible for multiple buildings and generally is not involved in day-to-day interaction with and education of students. The principal needs to ensure that students with disabilities are receiving the services they need, and that regulations and guidelines are being followed.

If you find that a student is not receiving the type of services required and delineated, you must respond in a timely manner. You may need to arrange a meeting to reevaluate the student or the student's education plan, or may have to consider corrective action plans for teachers who are not complying with students' special education plans.

The Principal Should Lead Efforts for Data Collection

In special education's infancy (1970s–1980s), there was no real expectation for keeping data on whether a student with a disability was making progress. Now, however, states—and, thus, individual schools—are required to make sure students with disabilities are making progress and that they are working towards achieving their goals and objectives. The only way to determine if a student is making progress is through data collection.

Data collection does not have to be an all-encompassing part of a teacher's job, but all teachers need to be able to demonstrate that what they are doing results in positive changes for students. If they cannot demonstrate that their instruction is supporting student progress, then teachers need to make the changes necessary to do so. Regular, consistent data collection is imperative to determine if students are making progress.

> All parents—whether their children are educated in the general education classroom or require special education services—need to receive regular, timely progress updates on the status of their children's efforts.

The Principal Should Ensure That All Staff Members Are Aware of the Process for Identifying Students With Disabilities

Most students with disabilities are not identified as eligible for special education and related services until they are in school, and the general education teacher is often the one who first notices the problems a child is having. Make sure that all general education teachers know what to look out for, that they keep other staff and parents informed of any concerns, and that they continually try their best to provide appropriate services for these students. It is essential to keep families informed of the progress students are making in the classroom, especially if a child is struggling or may be evaluated for special education services. Parents (and others) do not like surprises. Keep them informed of how students are doing, and of any special efforts being made on their behalf.

In addition, support staff in the cafeteria, on the bus, on the playground, or in school safety roles should know to report to supervisors any concerns they have about a child. Students with disabilities need services not just for academic problems, but also for social ones as well. It is often in unstructured settings that students with behavioral and social problems have the most difficulty.

The Principal Must Be Prepared to Lead Meetings Related to Services for Students With Disabilities

In order for students with disabilities to receive services, a representative of the school district with the authority to commit funds is required to be in attendance at any meeting and to oversee the process. Principals are increasingly being identified to serve in these roles. Therefore, the principal must understand what makes a child eligible for special education services (and what type of services), and be familiar with the regulations governing meetings (e.g., when to arrange meetings, what procedures to follow). Appendix B provides the federal definitions of various disability categories.

Parents and teachers look to the principal for leadership. Make sure you understand the roles of everyone involved in a student's education, and all the options that potentially may be discussed. One of your responsibilities is to supervise those who are providing special education services, so you must be knowledgeable about the general education curriculum, special education services available in the building, and resources available in the district and surrounding region.

The Principal Needs to Know All Students in the Building and Be Ready to Talk About Them

All families expect the principal to know their children and to understand each child's abilities and challenges. Observe all your students in the classroom, in the hallway, and in other settings. Child study meetings, teacher assistance team meetings, crisis team meetings, grade-level or content-area team meetings, and other collaborative groups all offer ways to learn about potential issues and challenges and to identify students who may be struggling. Talk with teachers about their students, make a practice of observing teachers in the classroom, and familiarize yourself with student records; you will oftentimes need to know the history of a student's placement, education programs, and supports. Remember, parents expect leadership from a principal and you will not be able to knowledgeably discuss students you do not know and have not observed.

You also need to be sensitive to the feelings and reactions of parents and students when discussing disabilities. Using "people-first" language (see box) is a way to convey that you recognize the student first, and the disability as a component or aspect of the student's personality. As a principal, you are in a unique position to shape the public image of people with disabilities. By putting the person first and using these suggested words, you can convey a positive, objective view of an individual instead of a negative, insensitive image.

People-First Language

People-first language is intended to offset earlier habits of dehumanizing individuals with disabilities ...

Instead of ...	*Say ...*
Differently abled, challenged	Disability
The disabled, handicapped	People with disabilities
Autistic	Person with autism, on the autism spectrum
Confined to a wheelchair	Uses a wheelchair
Slow learner	Has a learning disability
Brain-damaged	Has a brain injury
Retarded, mental retardation	Intellectual disability
Birth defect	Congenital disability
Seeing-eye dog	Service animal or dog

Talking with staff members prior to meetings also can alert you to other issues that might be raised. The purpose of the meeting might be to reevaluate a student's IEP, but the parents may have (and want to discuss) concerns about the aide in the classroom or the amount of homework a teacher is assigning.

The Principal Needs to Know How to Prevent Discipline Problems

Discipline is much more than dealing with students who have had problems; it should also be considered as a way to prevent problems from occurring. Principals should understand how to conduct and interpret functional behavior assessments (FBA)—and not just for students with disabilities. An FBA assesses the possible reasons for the way a student is behaving; the goal is to reduce or eliminate behaviors before they become problems. Prevention is much easier than having to deal with the consequence of a negative action.

Challenges Facing Principals

Significant changes have occurred over the past decade in the way special education services are provided to students with disabilities. Federal mandates (i.e., the No Child Left Behind Act of 2001 and reauthorizations of the Individuals With Disabilities Education Act), and trends in state and national curriculum standards (i.e., Common Core State Standards) continue to redefine requirements and goals. The present climate of school restructuring is placing new leadership demands on all administrators, especially principals. In addition, the move to educate students with disabilities in more inclusive settings necessitates shared responsibility and schoolwide collaboration—among supervisors, principals, general and special education teachers, and related service personnel.

The principal's responsibilities are time consuming. Everyone (teachers and families) assumes that the principal is the one with the greatest expertise in educational matters; however, there are few places to which principals can turn for help when making these types of

> *To be effective, today's school leaders must be knowledgeable about programs for students with disabilities and must provide appropriate support to teachers.*

decisions. And, unfortunately, most new principals come to their positions not as prepared as they need to be in special education matters.

The Council for Exceptional Children (CEC) realizes the great pressure that many principals feel when working with students in special education and their teachers. There is also an acknowledged continuing nationwide problem in recruiting and retaining special education teachers (Keigher & Cross, 2010). CEC (1998) developed a list of strategies that can assist principals in improving the working conditions of special education teachers (see box, "Strategies for Retaining and Supporting Staff"). Principals can use these strategies—which dovetail with the underlying themes of this guide—to develop an environment that supports all education staff members.

The Principal as Chief Advocate for Special Education

The principal sets the tone for the school community. Effective special education practices and an environment that supports all students' learning is a process that may take several years to evolve, but one that will be rewarding for all involved.

The foundation for this effort is the first theme we identified: *The principal is responsible for the education of all students in the school.* Share this ideal with your staff, and have them help you develop a school mission, vision, and core belief statements. Present this to a work group of parents and teachers, and ask them to assist you in developing an action plan for achieving your goals. Express this overarching idea of inclusion by planning schoolwide activities that celebrate acceptance, belonging, and diversity. Take the time to evaluate your mission and progress toward your goals throughout the school year, and learn about special education services, terms, and vocabulary (see Appendix C for a list of commonly used acronyms).

Strategies for Retaining and Supporting Staff

Present the attitude, "I want you to be here. You are important."

Be supportive of teacher decisions.

Encourage special and general educators to collaborate through teams and cooperative teaching opportunities. Experiment with multi-age classrooms and cross-curricular integration.

Ensure that there are mentoring programs in place throughout an educator's professional development.

Reward teachers with appropriate mechanisms.

Ensure that all education professionals are treated equitably.

Ensure that paraprofessionals and instructional aides are qualified and are consistently evaluated.

Provide time for teachers to plan.

Provide teachers with opportunities for professional development and opportunities to work on schoolwide committees. Workshops on collaboration, cooperative learning, teaming, assessment, adaptations, strategy instruction, and content enhancement may be beneficial.

Evaluate staff consistently to ensure that job demands are consistent with the knowledge, interests, and skills of employees.

Ensure that all education professionals have access to materials and resources, including the how-to's of school administrative practices.

Note. Adapted from *Retention of Special Education Professionals: A Practical Guide of Strategies and Activities for Educators and Administrators.* Copyright 1998 by the Council for Exceptional Children.

Let another theme guide your efforts: *Know all the students in the building and be ready to talk about them.* Listen to the dreams of your students' families. Never say "never," never say "always," and never say, "We don't do that here." As you work with parents, students, and teachers, continue to promote inclusion and student independence: focus on tasks and goals that are age-appropriate for students, and pursue "least restrictive" education settings for students with special education needs. Do not be fearful of trying inclusion activities that might seem impossible for the child to accomplish. You are in a stronger position if you have tried to meet the needs of the family and child by documenting that you have tried to implement a program in an inclusive setting.

As with any evolutionary process, special education requires a strong foundation. It is essential in the beginning years to place students with disabilities in classrooms with teachers who are positive, flexible, enthusiastic about trying, and caring. You can enhance the inclusion process by ensuring that all teachers and support staff know their roles and your expectations, while providing the support they need to in turn help students progress and access the curriculum.

Cultivating an Inclusive Environment

An inclusive environment is one in which students with disabilities are fully integrated into the school and its community. In this type of environment, every member of the school staff knows what is necessary for providing special education services, appropriately implements services for students with disabilities, and is aware of required processes and procedures.

An inclusive environment includes both tangible and intangible elements. As a principal, you may not have control over the structure of your building; however, you can ensure that students with disabilities are educated in classrooms in the mainstream of the school, that all areas of the school are accessible to those with physical disabilities, that all teachers implement procedures for routine activities that support students with disabilities, and that students with disabilities receive support that encourages them to be as independent as possible.

In creating an inclusive environment, ensure that students with disabilities have equal access to and are invited and encouraged to participate in all extracurricular activities (e.g., sports and clubs), field trips, and social activities. Encouraging students with disabilities to participate in clubs and sports will help them to feel a part of the school community. To ensure that they participate equally with their typically developing peers, however, you may need to ensure dignity in participation (i.e., watch carefully for patronizing) and provide support services (e.g., sign-language interpretators, aides). The practice of including students with disabilities in all aspects of school life should extend throughout their time in your elementary or secondary school. In this country, there is a wide range of diploma options for students with disabilities; regardless of the type of program in which a student is enrolled, or the type of certificate or diploma students receive, they should have the opportunity to fully participate in any graduation ceremonies and culminating events.

Modifications, Accommodations, and Testing

One of the most controversial issues in inclusive education is making modifications to the curriculum for student success. Many teachers and parents worry that accommodating special student needs "dumbs down" the system. It is important that when you develop your school's inclusion mission statement and goals, this is an area where there is consensus. All teaching staff should be in agreement with and follow the same procedures for reporting progress for students with disabilities, for administering alternate and alternative assessments, and for implementing appropriate classroom accommodations.

Students' special education plans should always include a statement or description of whether and how the student will participate in standardized testing. Review each student's strengths and needs (as well as governing regulations) to determine whether the standardized assessment will accurately evaluate the student's progress and to what extent the student can participate. In addition to ensuring that your school routinely offers commonly used accommodations such as extended time and small-group testing, you may need to explore training in your state's alternative assessment procedures for individual staff members.

In the pages that follow, you will be able to explore many of these areas in greater depth. The appendices to this book include tools and information to support principals in all of these areas: There is a listing of common education acronyms and abbreviations, definitions of different types of disabilities, and other material to support you in developing processes for assessment of students with disabilities and providing special education services to them.

People with disabilities inhabit all phases of our lives and our communities. Our job as educators is to create settings and programs that will enable everyone— including those who have disabilities—to be able maximize their chances for rich and happy lives.

What Does a Principal Need to Know About Special Education Law?

This chapter discusses the main laws affecting special education. It provides an overview of the Individuals With Disabilities Education Act (IDEA), Sections 504 and 508 of the Rehabilitation Act of 1973, the Americans With Disabilities Act (ADA) and its amendments, and the Family Educational Rights and Privacy Act (FERPA). Each of these laws provides guidance for educating students with disabilities, and each is important for principals to understand.

Quick Points

- The main law governing special education is IDEA (2006). It covers identification, placement, and services.

- Students with disabilities are entitled to an appropriate education.

- Students with disabilities are to be educated in the least restrictive environment.

- Not all students with disabilities are eligible for special education services under IDEA; Section 504 plans provide education accommodations and modifications for these students.

- Section 508 governs accessibility of technology and online programs for students with disabilities.

- FERPA governs who can see documents relating to a student.

Special education law is constantly changing due to litigation and legislative attempts to solve problems. However, it is very important for principals to keep up to date about changing requirements. The following information follows the themes delineated in the Introduction: The principal is responsible for the education of all students in the school, and the principal needs to be versed in special education topics and approaches. One of the most important components of special education is the legal aspect. Understanding the laws will go a long toward ensuring students with disabilities receive the education they need.

The Individuals With Disabilities Education Act (IDEA)

IDEA is the main law governing the educational rights of eligible students with disabilities in school. According to federal law, every child with a disability is entitled to a free appropriate public education (FAPE). The original title of IDEA was the Education for All Handicapped Children's Act (Pub. L. No. 94-142, 1975). Congress chose that title to emphasize how important it was for all children to be included. At the time, public schools had routinely excluded (and many were still excluding) children with disabilities because they were perceived as not being able to benefit from education or as not being "ready" for school. By passing the Education for All Handicapped Children's Act, Congress wanted to make the point that no child was to be excluded.

Identification, Evaluation, and Placement

Historically, there have been problems in the testing and placement of children with disabilities (e.g., not testing students in their primary language, not measuring adaptive behavior, relying on a single test for classification and placement). These practices resulted in court cases stipulating correct procedures for the assessment and classification of children with disabilities, including:

- All children are to be tested in their primary language.
- IQ tests alone cannot be used for the placement of children into special education programs.
- Unvalidated tests and group tests are not to be used for determining eligibility.
- Parents must be notified before any testing may begin.
- Adaptive behavior must be taken into account when considering eligibility.
- A district must seek out and evaluate each child with a suspected disability in its jurisdiction.
- Districts need to implement procedures to screen preschool-age children for disabilities.

State and local education agencies are required by IDEA to actively seek out and identify students with disabilities who require special education services. School districts must make public their procedures for identifying and evaluating students; this might include announcements in the newspaper, as well as notices in grocery stores, gas stations, physician's offices, and churches, or "informational brochures, … public service announcements, [and] staffing exhibits at health fairs and other community activities" (34 C.F.R. § 300.131[c]). Notices should include dates and locations for screening to determine eligibility for services before entering school at age 5 or 6. Regardless of the age of the child, school districts must identify the specific nature of a child's disability and determine the type and extent of special education and related services required.

In addition, any evaluation of a child must be an *individualized assessment* of all areas related to the suspected disability. This means that if the child has a suspected reading disability, the assessment focuses on reading; if the suspected problem is a math disability, the focus is on math. A team (rather than a single individual) must make the eligibility decision, with at least one member of the team experienced in the suspected disability category. The job of the team is to determine whether a child is eligible for special education and related services. (For more on eligibility for special education services, see Chapter 3.) Note that districts also must notify parents of their right to an independent evaluation at public expense if they disagree with the results or procedures of the school district's evaluation (34 C.F.R. § 300.502).

> *The IEP is a legal document describing the special education and related services designed to meet the needs of a child who has a disability.*

IDEA defines *children with disabilities* as those with autism, deaf-blindness, deafness, developmental delay, emotional disturbance, hearing impairment, intellectual disability, multiple disabilities, orthopedic impairment, other health impairment, specific learning disability, speech or language impairment, traumatic brain injury, or visual impairment (including blindness; see Appendix B for definitions). Note that for students to be eligible for special education and related services as a "child with a disability" under one of these categories, the student's educational performance must be adversely affected due to the disability (34 CFR § 300.8[a][2][i]).

If the evaluation team finds the student eligible for special education, they must develop an individualized education program (IEP) based on the results of the assessments. The IEP includes a statement of the child's present level of educational performance and goals and objectives based on this functioning. It also describes in detail how services will be provided (e.g., placement, dates and duration of services, related services), objective criteria and evaluation procedures, and schedules for determining progress toward IEP goals.

(For more on IEPs, see Chapter 4.) If the team decides that the student is not going to be educated alongside students without disabilities, documentation is necessary stating why this will not occur, and when such placement might occur.

The IEP is more than just a document outlining goals and objectives. It serves as a written commitment by the local education agency to provide the services. Because in years past many children were placed inappropriately in special education and remained there for the duration of their schooling, IDEA mandates at least a 3-year or triennial reevaluation, to determine whether a child still qualifies for special education services (34 CFR § 300.303[a]).

Appropriate Education

Historically, students with disabilities were placed in a disability-specific classroom, whether or not that placement would provide them an "appropriate" education. The term *appropriate*, however, continues to cause confusion. What one parent, supervisor, principal, or teacher finds appropriate, another might deem completely inappropriate.

For state and local education agencies to receive federal funding for special education, they need to show they are providing an appropriate education for all students with disabilities in their jurisdiction. Districts demonstrate this through the development of an IEP. The definition of appropriate education is a process definition: If the district follows a certain process in the development and implementation of the IEP, then the student should be receiving an acceptable result. This is why it is imperative that principals have a full and complete understanding of the IEP process and need to become an active participant. The principal is ultimately responsible to ensure not only that the district is following appropriate procedures, but also that students are receiving an appropriate education (see box, "Questions to Guide Determination of 'Appropriate Education'").

Because defining appropriate education focuses on the process, the burden is on the professionals who develop and implement the IEP to verify and be able to show that it was based on correct information. Districts also need to be able to show an IEP was properly developed and implemented, and that proper monitoring occurred during its implementation.

Least Restrictive Environment

The last question in the list to guide evaluation of appropriate placement of students relates to the extent to which students with disabilities are included in classrooms with their typically developing peers (see also Chapter 5). IDEA specifies that, "to the maximum extent appropriate," students with disabilities are educated with students without disabilities (20 U.S.C. §20 U.S. Code § 1412[a][5][A]). The current term for this in special education is inclusion. The presumption is that students with disabilities will be educated in general education classrooms with supports, unless it can be shown the child cannot benefit from education in this setting.

Because special education is determined by services provided rather than setting, schools must be prepared to offer

> a continuum of alternative placements ... to meet the needs of children with disabilities for special education and related services ([including] instruction in regular classes, special classes, special schools, home instruction, and instruction in hospitals and institutions); and make provision for supplementary services (such as resource room or itinerant instruction) to be provided in conjunction with regular class placement. (34 C.F.R. 300.115[a]–[b])

Again, the specific services to be provided and in what format must be described in the IEP.

Questions to Guide Determination of "Appropriate Education"

- Was the student evaluated in a nondiscriminatory fashion?
- Are all members of the IEP team certified for their roles in the development and implementation of the IEP?
- Is the IEP truly individualized? Is it specifically designed to meet the needs of this particular student?
- Are the necessary related services listed?
- Are all the components listed for service on the IEP being implemented?
- Is there clear documentation on the level of functioning of the student in comparison to the goals and objectives on the IEP?
- Is the student receiving educational benefit from the program?
- Are all the objectives of the IEP behaviorally written?
- Have the parents or guardians been involved in every step of the development of the IEP?
- Have the parents or guardians been made aware of their due process rights?
- Is the student integrated with typically developing peers to the maximum extent possible? If there is no current provision for integration, is there a plan for this in the future?

Often forgotten is that the law stipulates services are to follow students; that is, services are to be tailored to the unique needs of the individual in the most appropriate setting. It is not acceptable for students to be assigned services solely designated for a particular disability or to programs that are available or convenient. Just because a student is identified as having severe intellectual disability does not mean the student has to be placed in a self-contained classroom when a partial-day program or a resource room might be a more appropriate option for that child. Every school district needs to have available a continuum of services spanning everything between the general education classroom and hospital-type settings.

Shared Decision Making

For a long time, parents were shut out of the decision-making process, partly because it was assumed that they were the cause of the child's disability (e.g., Bruno Bettelheim's early theories about autism). Professionals knew what was best for the children and viewed parents as ignorant of their children's educational needs. Families, however, have essential information about their children with disabilities. IDEA recognizes this, and requires that schools ensure parental participation throughout the special education process–specifying procedures for notification, access to records, consultation, and participation in advisory panels.

Shared decision making protects the rights of students by ensuring that someone involved in the process has a long-term interest in the child. It also can be argued that what affects the student with a disability also affects the parents; therefore, most educators regard parents as important stakeholders. Thus, parents need to be aware of—and consent to—every step of the process. This process includes the initial evaluation, the eligibility meeting, the development of the IEP, the annual review, and the reevaluation process. Families also need access to all the records kept on their children and the assurances about confidentiality.

In addition, amendments to IDEA have added requirements for parent involvement: districts must establish a public awareness campaign, a comprehensive child-find program, and a central director of information. School systems have a legal obligation to work with families when children are identified as needing special education services.

Note that this effort extends to preschool children as well (20 U.S.C. 1435[a] [5]); the goal is to provide children with as much assistance as possible before they enter school for the first time. School districts must be prepared to develop an individualized family services plan (IFSP) for preschool-age children who are deemed eligible. Similar to the development of the IEP, the IFSP includes a heavy family component. The IFSP should describe supports for the other family members, to help them meet the needs of their child with a disability; this might include training family members to carry out specific duties, or collaborating with them to determine the best methods for working with the child. The IFSP is more than just an IEP with a family twist, though: It is a multidisciplinary document designed to enhance children's development and minimize developmental delays by enhancing the family's capacity to meet the child's needs.

Another important component of the early childhood amendments is the realization that one service provider does not have to be the only one working to address circumstances for the child with a disability and related family members. Ideally, multiple agencies must work together to provide a combination of approaches and interventions.

Due Process

As noted previously, IDEA requires parental involvement at all the different levels affecting a child's eligibility for special education services. If parents or guardians disapprove of the methods used for determining eligibility and educational programming for children with disabilities or disapprove of the resulting decisions, due process procedures (established by the Fifth and 14th Amendments of the Constitution) allow them to challenge the school system.

Appropriate notification is one essential element of procedural due process. IDEA is very specific about requirements relating to notice, requiring written notice before schools can propose (or refuse) to initiate or change "the identification, evaluation, or educational placement of the child" or the provision of an appropriate education (34 C.F.R. § 300.503[a]–[b]). Schools also must convey the details of the proposed action and the reasons for the action.

Parents may request a due process hearing if they are not happy with any or all aspects of the procedures or the education of their child with a disability. The purpose of the due process hearing is to resolve differences of opinion between parents and school officials regarding the education, placement, or services for the child with a disability. If the parents request a hearing, a hearing officer independent of the local education agency conducts the hearing. The hearing is at a time and place suitable to the parents.

A due process hearing tends to be an antagonistic process. It usually ends with both parties unhappy about the results or feeling they received less than they wanted. Although due process hearings require an enormous amount of energy, time, and money, due process procedures are an invaluable means of ensuring an appropriate education and the participation of parents in the education of their children.

Instead of due process hearings, more individuals and school systems are using another form of resolution: mediation. Mediation involves the use of less formal, less adversarial, more negotiated-settlement meetings for resolving disputes. Usually in mediation, a neutral party hears the issues and helps parties find an acceptable solution. There has been a significant increase in the number of cases using mediation (Rothstein & Johnson, 2013).

Related Services

In addition to the educational services students with disabilities receive, they may require other, additional services to fully benefit from special education. These *related services* include

> transportation and such developmental, corrective, and other supportive services as are required to assist a child with a disability to benefit from special education, [such as] speech-language pathology and audiology services, interpreting services, psychological services, physical and occupational therapy, recreation, including therapeutic recreation, early identification and assessment of disabilities in children, counseling services, including rehabilitation counseling, orientation and mobility services, and medical services for diagnostic or evaluation purposes. Related services also include school health services and school nurse services, social work services in schools, and parent counseling and training. (34 C.F.R. § 300.34[a])

Several conditions must be met before students receive related services. First, to be entitled to related services a child must be eligible for special education services. Unfortunately, there are students who might benefit from these related services but because they are not eligible for special education they cannot receive related services; in the absence of this eligibility, the student does not qualify for related services. Second, only those services necessary for the student to benefit from special education may be provided, regardless of how easily a school nurse or lay person could furnish them. For example, if a particular medication or treatment may appropriately be administered to a child other than during the school day, the school is not required to provide nursing services to administer. Third, the regulations state that medical services must be provided only if they can be performed by a nurse or other qualified person, not if a physician is required (34 C.F.R. § 300.34).

As discussed previously, any initial evaluation for special education eligibility must be sufficiently comprehensive so as to identify all of the student's education-related needs, including related services—whether or not those needs are commonly linked to the particular disability category. Goals can be written for a related service just as they are for other special education services. The IEP also must specify, with respect to each service, when the service will begin, how often it will be provided and for what amount of time, and where it will be provided (34 C.F.R. § 300.320[a][7]).

Not all students with disabilities require related services. Further, the preceding list of related services from the federal regulations is not exhaustive and may include other developmental, corrective, or supportive services if they are required for the student to benefit from special education (e.g., artistic and cultural programs; art, music, and dance therapy).

School districts may not charge parents of eligible students with disabilities for the costs of related services that have been included on the IEP. Just as special education services must be provided to an eligible student with a disability at no cost to the parent or guardian, so too must related services when the IEP team has determined that such services are required. The need for related services should be determined in the same manner as classroom placement (i.e., as appropriate to the individual student) and listed on the IEP. Finally, IDEA requires school districts to provide any related services identified as needed by the student, regardless of whether they are available at the time of IEP development.

> *It is the IEP team's responsibility to review all of the evaluation information, to identify any related services the child needs, and to include them in the IEP.*

Transition Services

Many of the changes in governing disability law, including special education law, over the years were a result of learning the lessons of history: Students with disabilities in many cases were leaving a free appropriate public education and entering a system where there were no mandates, and students educated in special education were not achieving desired outcomes. Thus, IDEA defines *transition services* as

> a coordinated set of activities for a student designed within an outcome-oriented process that promotes movement from school to post-school activities, including postsecondary education, vocational training, integrated employment (including supported employment), continuing and adult education, adult services, independent living, or community participation. The coordinated set of activities must be based upon the individual student's needs, taking into account

the student's preferences and interests, and must include instruction, community experiences, the development of employment and other post-school adult living objectives, and, if appropriate, acquisition of daily living skills and functional vocational evaluation. Transition services must promote or facilitate the achievement of the employment outcome identified in the student's individualized plan for employment. (34 C.F.R. § 361.5[b][55])

For parents to be integrally involved in assisting their teens in making informed choices, they also need information about transition services. Schools must provide families with information and training sessions offering topical subjects such as postsecondary education options, work-force issues, independent living, finance planning, and agency involvement. Embedded in these sessions should be the concept that once the student leaves public school, the service delivery system changes dramatically: Young adults with disabilities and their families must move from a familiar system within the public schools into an unfamiliar and uncertain adult services system. Moreover, unlike the educational system, which entitles all children to receive services, the adult service system requires eligibility. Parents need to prepare for this reality and the possible limitations of adult services—and this means developing informal relationships with those who might provide services.

The Rehabilitation Act of 1973

There are some students with disabilities who do not need special education (i.e., adapted curriculum). For example, a student who is missing a leg due a car accident and is doing fine in school both educationally and socially has a disability but does not need the support of a special education teacher. A student who has breathing problems due to a reaction to certain chemicals, and is doing fine in school both academically and socially, clearly has a disability but does not need special education. Some students with ADD/ADHD are considered to have a disability, but often do not require the support of a special education teacher. These individuals all have disabilities, but are not eligible for special education services. Their needs, however, are accommodated by Section 504 of the Rehabilitation Act of 1973 (Section 504, 2009). Table 1.1 provides an overview of the primary differences between IDEA and Section 504.

Table 1.1 Differences Between IDEA and Section 504		
Focus	IDEA	Section 504
Main purpose	To ensure a free appropriate public education for students with disabilities who are identified as meeting the requirements of one of 13 disability categories.	To prevent discrimination against students with disabilities in agencies or organizations receiving federal funds.
Who is protected?	Eligible students with disabilities ages 3–21 who require specially designed instruction to benefit from education.	A *person with a disability,* that is, someone who • has a physical or mental impairment which limits one or more major life activities; • has a record of such an impairment; or • is regarded as having an impairment.
Services provided	Free special education services to support students with disabilities in their access of the general education curriculum when appropriate.	No special education services; schools are required to make sure that students can participate in school (i.e., education and activities) without discrimination.

Section 504

Section 504—which was subsumed under the ADA Amendments Act of 2008 (discussion to follow)—is focused on anti-discrimination. Section 504's intent is to protect students' civil rights, ensuring equal access and preventing discrimination—which is different from establishing eligibility for special education services. The main component of Section 504 states:

> No otherwise qualified individual with a disability in the United States … shall, solely by reason of her or his disability, be excluded from the participation in, be denied the benefits of, or be subjected to discrimination under any program or activity receiving Federal financial assistance. (29 U.S.C. § 794[a])

Section 504, therefore, protects from discrimination students who have "a physical or mental impairment which substantially limits one or more major life activities, … [have] a record of such an impairment, or … [are] regarded as having such an impairment" (34 C.F.R. § 104.3[j][1]). For the purposes of Section 504, *major life activities* include "functions such as caring for one's self, performing manual tasks, walking, seeing, hearing, speaking, breathing, learning, and working" (34 C.F.R. § 104.3[j][2][ii]). The law protects individuals from both intentional and unintentional discrimination. Under Section 504, individuals who have a disability can qualify for a related service necessary for them to benefit from education. In addition, Section 504 has provisions for non-discriminatory employment.

Because principals are often involved in the development of Section 504 plans, they need to be familiar with the types of accommodations typically provided for students with disabilities who are not eligible for special education services under IDEA. In addition to general accommodations (see Table 1.2), certain accommodations and services might be considered for specific disability profiles. These types of general accommodations when implemented promote a "universally designed" classroom, increasing accessibility to content for all students. Not all accommodations will be necessary or beneficial to a student, but it is always helpful to be prepared and focused on what is possible or might be needed. Appendix D provides some additional examples of classroom accommodations that might be appropriate for students eligible under Section 504, and which relate to specific disabilities or disorders.

An accommodation is any technique that alters the academic setting or environment in some way, but does not change the content of required work. A modification is any technique that alters the work required in such a way that it differs in substance from the work required of other students in the same class.

Section 508

Section 508, also originally part of the Rehabilitation Act of 1973 (later incorporated into the Workforce Investment Act of 1998), requires that electronic and information technology developed, procured, maintained, or used by the federal government be accessible to people with disabilities. This requirement also applies to any states that receive funding through the Technology Related Assistance for Individuals with Disabilities Act of 1988.

When evaluating incorporating technology into the education program—whether via increased use of computers, laptops, or tablets in the classroom or online or "flipped" learning—principals need to ensure that students with disabilities are afforded equal access to the material. Equal access includes not only adaptations for students with physical disabilities, but also considerations of content accessibility, for example, for students with learning disabilities. (See Appendix A for resources and information on students with disabilities and online learning environments.)

Table 1.2 General Section 504 Accommodations	
Environmental	Structured learning environment
	A separate "space" for different types of tasks
	Preferential seating (e.g., closer to teacher)
	Study carrels
	Easier access to personal/classroom supplies to minimize distractions
	Sensory breaks
	Written or picture schedules/task analysis
	Reinforce use of compensatory strategies
Organizational	Model and reinforce organizational systems
	Written assignments/check student's recording of assignments
	Schedule/milestones for assignments
	Clear beginning/end times for activities/assignments
	Direct instruction of study and organizational skills
	Before- and after-school tutoring/homework assistance
Behavioral	Use behavioral management techniques consistently within classroom, across classes, and schoolwide
	Implement behavioral/academic contracts
	Utilize positive verbal and nonverbal reinforcements, logical consequences
	Home–school communication system
	Post rules and consequences for classroom behavior
	Maintain daily/weekly progress reports and contracts
	Reinforce self-monitoring

Table 1.2 (continued) General Section 504 Accommodations	
Presentation	Provide alternate presentation of information (e.g., audio, visual), alternate choice of texts/sources
	Incorporate technology aids
	Provide guided notes, outlines, study guides
	Prioritize drill and practice activities for relevance
	Vary lesson presentation methods (visual demonstrations, collaborative group work, computer-assisted instruction, peer tutors, experiments, games)
	Check student understanding by asking students to repeat/paraphrase
	Match materials to student level of understanding/skills and preferred learning style
	Pre-teach and reteach important concepts
Assignment modifications	Modify amount of homework
	Supplement oral instructions with written directions
	Permit student choice in method of presentation
	Break assignments into smaller steps
Testing and assessment accommodations	Consider test-question presentation (amount of material on a single page, readability/accessibility)
	Provide sample or practice tests
	Read-aloud/scribe
	Provide tests in segments so that student hands in one segment before receiving the next part
	Untimed exams/extended time for completing tests
	Modify weights of tests when grading

The Americans With Disabilities Act

Though the Rehabilitation Act was passed in 1973, individuals with disabilities continued, as a group, to occupy an inferior status in our society, and were severely disadvantaged socially, vocationally, economically, and educationally. Congress strengthened the law through its subsequent amendments and with the passage of the Americans With Disabilities Act of 1990 (ADA, Pub. L. No. 101-336, 1990). In 2008, the Americans With Disabilities Act Amendments Act (ADAAA, 2009) broadened the parameters of the original ADA. ADAAA included a "conforming amendment" to Section 504, meaning that the newly expanded coverage under ADAAA also applied to Section 504. Although ADAAA retained existing definitions of *disability* and *impairment*, it expanded the definition of *major life activities* to include bodily functions and spelled out the rules of construction for *substantial limitation*. The reason for this was that Congress felt that the previous standard was too hard to meet, resulting in discrimination.

Section 504 of the Rehabilitation Act and the ADA are broader and more inclusive than IDEA. For example, many students with physical disabilities do not require special assistance to access the curriculum, and therefore are not classified as needing special education services. However, they still meet the definition of having a disability under the Section 504. Therefore, not providing reasonable accommodations to enable these students to fully participate in activities, events, or classes is discriminatory and illegal.

The ADA strives for "equality of opportunity, full participation, independent living, and economic self-sufficiency" (42 U.S.C. § 12101[a][8]) for persons with disabilities. The main purpose of the ADA is to provide civil rights to the 43 million Americans with disabilities who have been unable to access their communities and necessary services. Critics argue that the ADA prevents businesses from expanding and wrecks small business. However, its main interest is to promote equal access and freedom for people with disabilities. Others state the ADA is an extension on the installment of a contract between individuals with disabilities, their family members, and the government for a lifetime of services and accessibility that starts with special education services received in schools. The intent of the ADA is to open more of society to people with disabilities; in practice, the Act is changing the norms of society.

Like IDEA, Section 504 and the ADA allow statutory venues for remediation of complaints. This provides individuals with disabilities and their families an avenue through which they can file complaints against public schools. If these complaints are valid, schools potentially face the loss of federal funds.

The Family Educational Rights and Privacy Act

The Family Educational Rights and Privacy Act of 1974 (FERPA, 2006) defines who may and may not see student records. There are several major points that are important to consider relating to FERPA:

1. FERPA guarantees the parents or guardians of a student the right to inspect and review their child's records.

2. FERPA establishes policies through which parents can challenge the accuracy of student records.

3. FERPA establishes a mechanism through which parents can appeal concerning alleged failures to comply with the law.

4. FERPA prohibits the release of information about a student without the parents' or guardians' consent, except to those who have a legitimate right to know.

5. Districts need to establish a written policy about who will have access to student records.

As a principal, it is important to realize that all of the information obtained as a part of the assessment process to determine whether a student has a disability is to be placed in the student's file. The only exceptions to this may be the actual test protocols used by the individual administering the psychological and educational assessments. In addition, student files should include evaluation reports, IEPs, and summaries of progress toward IEP goals and objectives.

The important component about FERPA is that all of a student's records are located in the files, parents have access to them, they can challenge them, and the files contain confidential information. Knowing this, all school principals should be very judicious about who has access. In addition, it is necessary to safeguard the files, and ensure the appropriate information remains in the files.

Quick Review

This chapter has provided an overview of the laws related to the education of students with disabilities. It is very important, as a principal, to have the knowledge required to ensure that students with disabilities receive appropriate services—and equally important to ensure your staff members know what is necessary for special education.

What Does a Principal Need to Know About Staffing?

Good quality staff can make or break a program. Principals need to know what questions to ask when hiring, and how to support new and veteran special education staff. Other chapters in this book highlight the role of the principals as instructional leader and how to monitor special education teachers and provide accountability. This chapter highlights the importance of choosing and supporting effective special and general education staff.

Quick Points

- Take time to hire staff. They will carry your program.
- Learn the requirements of the special education jobs in your building and work to match staff credentials as much as possible.
- Try to find staff who can work with general education teachers.

Selecting staff to teach students with disabilities is not a consideration limited to hiring special education teachers and paraprofessionals or instructional aides. The needs of students with disabilities should to be considered when hiring all general education teachers, assistant principals, classroom assistants, resource personnel, and support staff—because your students will interact with all of these staff members. Every staff member should have high expectations for all students, have some knowledge of the laws governing special education (see Chapter 1), accept students with all types of disabilities, and be familiar with current best practices in teaching and instructional strategies. A carefully planned staff development program is helpful in filling any gaps. Your support staff might also include physical therapists, counselors, occupational therapists, nurses, vision specialists, mobility specialists, speech therapists, and non-English-language or sign language interpreters; best practices for hiring teaching staff apply to these members of your team as well.

Special Education Teachers

Special education teachers face unique challenges in the education environment (see Chapter 10). The gains their students make are often very small and come only after intense effort. They have to individualize instruction to find success, because they usually work with students who have widely varying needs. They need to listen to the concerns of parents who may be demanding, disinterested, or ungrateful (although most are conscientious and very thankful for the work of special educators). Some special education teachers feel isolated because their students are often a small percentage of the total school population and frequently left out of many aspects of the mainstream life of the school. Special education teachers meet these challenges on a daily basis because they care deeply, often passionately, about their students.

As a principal, you need to set the example to the rest of the staff that special education is an integral part of the educational program at your school. The key is establishing a philosophy integrating the special education component into decisions from the beginning, not as an afterthought. Not only do special education teachers sometimes feel disconnected from the rest of the staff, but general education teachers also often feel disconnected from special education teachers. The main idea to get across is that all teachers have more in common than they do differences. Special education teachers are teaching the same material and can benefit from the same inservice activities. Special education teachers can provide invaluable resources to staff members seeking strategies to use with struggling students, some of whom may have undiagnosed learning disabilities. General education teachers need to be able to adapt to differing learning styles, implement classroom accommodations, and use a variety

> *Special education teachers should communicate regularly with general education teachers about specific students, and take the time to listen to and discuss concerns.*

of teaching strategies—often as the first tier of instruction, for all students, before a student is ever evaluated for special education services.

Working with general education teachers before the first day of classes, the special education teacher can help them prepare for effectively including students with disabilities. For a long time, special education teachers wanted anonymity for these students, to give them a "fair" chance. For many reasons, anonymity is not the best plan; with IDEA requirements that at least one general education teacher participate on a student's individualized education program (IEP) team (34 CFR § 300.321[a][2]), it is also against the law. For your school to provide the best education for all students, general education teachers need as much information as is available. At a minimum, they need to be familiar with accommodations required by student IEPs, including any medical information or behavioral information pertaining to the classroom and learning—all of which are considered essential to student success in the classroom. If a student fails to progress, it is the responsibility of the special education teacher to schedule an IEP team meeting and discuss appropriate interventions for the student.

It is the responsibility of the principal to provide the structure and opportunities in which special education teachers can become a part of the total school experience, and develop an environment of acceptance and cooperation (see box, "Integrating Special Education Staff Into Schoolwide Activities"). Providing both direction and time will help your staff reach these goals.

Integrating Special Education Staff Into Schoolwide Activities

- Assign special education teachers as coaches and club sponsors, to serve on committees; encourage them to attend extracurricular activities and participate in professional development programs.

- Have a special education department teach a portion of the school's gifted and talented education program. At the secondary school level, explore possibilities of co-teaching in honors, AP, and IB classes.

- Ensure general education teachers learn about special education teachers' jobs, the special education program, and the types of student needs the program is addressing.

- Provide professional development activities for general education teachers on special education topics. Topics could include special education law, how to provide accommodations, how to participate in an IEP conference, and the special education process.

Managing Larger Special Education Populations by Co-Teaching

"Placement" for students with disabilities—as mentioned in Chapter 1 and as will be discussed more thoroughly in Chapter 6—refers to how schools provide special education services to students with disabilities. When a school's special education population is 10% or less of the total student population, typical inclusion and resource models may work well. In these typical models, a student is scheduled for at least one resource class with a special education teacher and all other classes in the general education classroom. However, when the special population exceeds 10% and approaches 15% or more, general education classes begin to reach critical mass with students with disabilities. Expecting a general education teacher to effectively manage a classroom of 30 students including 10 to 12 students needing special education is impractical. Implementing a co-teaching model can be beneficial to both students and staff.

Co-teaching does not mean that the special education teacher is an assistant in the general education classroom. In the most effective co-teaching model, both the general education teacher and the special education teacher provide classroom instruction. Once students see both teachers teaching, the teachers gain credibility and students are more open to learning and accepting help. Often, the biggest hurdle to overcome is the general education teacher's reluctance to "give up" class time to the special education teacher. For co-teaching to be effective, however, the special education teacher should carry out some or all of the following teaching responsibilities:

A co-teaching model utilizes the expertise of the general education teacher and special education teacher in the same classroom, working together to teach all students.

- Conduct the warm-up activity.
- Direct the independent practice activity.
- Conduct the review or summary at the end of the lesson.
- Assign homework.
- Conduct the homework review.

In this model, the general education teacher continues to deliver content, but the special education teacher also contributes to classroom instruction.

A special education teacher might co-teach one class or block a day, with the rest of the time in resource classrooms or self-contained instructional settings. One caution that must be noted is that in a school with a large special education population, co-teaching may result in increased resource class size. The benefits of students with disabilities being instructed in the general education classroom setting alongside their typically developing peers, however, far outweigh the drawback of slightly larger resource classes (see box, "Advantages of Co-Teaching").

One approach is to pair a special education teacher with two different teachers at different times during the school day. The special educator can co-teach in one class in the morning while a paraprofessional or instructional aide works with the other co-taught class, and then reverse their roles in the afternoon. In this scenario, then, this subject area would have four different co-taught, inclusive classes throughout the day. This has the benefit of raising the profile of co-teaching and making it a "normal" part of the school's education delivery process. It means, however, that the special educator needs time to plan with two or more other staff members. Collaborative planning is essential for seamless lesson delivery; scheduling a common planning time for these teachers is essential to the success of your program.

To launch a successful co-teaching program, select two teachers who are open to trying a new idea and who are less likely to be territorial about sharing a classroom (and students). Planning together and sharing classroom and instructional responsibilities requires the cooperation and flexibility of both teachers. Once it works well, other teachers will realize the benefits of co-teaching.

Advantages of Co-Teaching

- Sharing instructional strategies enhances the pedagogy of both teachers.

- Having two teachers in a classroom makes individual assistance available to more students; this also reduces discipline incidents.

- Marginal students—those who do not qualify for special education services—can receive the specialized assistance of a special education teacher.

- If either teacher is absent, the lesson planned for the day can continue without resorting to substitute lesson plans.

- Special education teachers become more confident with content areas, supporting their work with students during resource time.

- General education teachers learn more specialized instructional strategies that they can implement in their other classes.

Interviewing and Hiring Special Education Teachers

Often the supervisor of special education or your district's human resources office will have prepared questions for you to use when interviewing special education teacher candidates. Another approach is to convene an interview committee in advance of the interviews and decide on the topics to be covered and the questions; you can even decide who is going to ask which questions. Questions should cover qualifications, classroom management, technology expertise, individualized education program (IEP) development and implementation, communication with families, and collaborative practices (see Table 2.1; see also CEC's excellent resource, *What Every Special Educator Must Know*, 2009b).

Table 2.1
Interviewing Special Education Candidates: Sample Questions
General questions/statements
Please take a few minutes and tell us about yourself, especially your background in special education.
The position vacancy for which you are interviewing is (describe the position: elementary resource room teacher, high school special education specialist, full-time co-teacher in a general education elementary classroom or secondary content-area class, etc.). What course work or experiences in your background have prepared you to take on the responsibilities of this position?
If hired for this position, what would you do to establish or change the classroom environment (e.g., furniture arrangement, learning center displays, wall hangings and board displays)?
Describe the system of classroom management along with the rewards and consequences of that system that you consider appropriate for this particular position.
What is your usual approach to initiating and maintaining communication with students' families?
What ideas do you have for integrating students with disabilities in the general education curriculum?
What ideas do you have for including students with disabilities in a school's extracurricular activities?
How do you establish working relationships with general education teachers and support staff?
Describe your background in educational technology. Highlight specific pieces of equipment and software that you have used while taking course work and teaching students.

Table 2.1 (continued)
Interviewing Special Education Candidates: Sample Questions
Lesson planning, curriculum, assessment, and teaching strategies
Describe the essential elements of a good lesson plan
What kinds of (reading, math) programs and approaches have you been taught to use or have used in your teaching practice?
What approaches do you use when grouping students for small-group activities?
What types of classroom modifications or accommodations or curricular adaptations have you used to help students keep pace and successfully meet grade-level standards?
How do you interface with specialists (speech/language teachers, occupational therapists, physical therapists, vision specialists, hearing specialists, adaptive equipment/assistive technology specialists, behavior specialists, etc.) and how do you incorporate their suggestions and treatments into your planning and lesson execution?
What is a special education teacher's role regarding supportive, inclusionary instruction in the subject areas of math, language arts, science, and social studies?
What is a special education teacher's role concerning subjects such as art, music, technology, physical education, and library science?
When working with students in a resource room setting, how do you organize yourself and your students in order to meet all of their individual needs?
What specific standardized assessment tests do you feel confident in administering and scoring in order to obtain present educational levels for a student?
What kinds of informal assessment devices or techniques would you use to obtain present educational levels for a student?

No matter what questions you use, be sure you ask the same questions of each candidate; this gives every candidate the same chance to succeed. Having the same person ask the same question(s) also helps to maintain uniformity. When interviewing potential candidates, your committee should not be too large or too small; generally, between three and six people, and representative of your special education staff, your general education staff, and your administration. This does not preclude asking follow-up questions to obtain specific information about an area of experience or expertise that a particular candidate may have. However, by using a set of standard questions for all candidates, the committee members will have universal points of reference when narrowing down the candidates for either selection recommendations or follow-up interviews.

The number of questions asked during the interviews will depend upon the amount of time you have scheduled for each interview. If the interview committee is a screening committee rather than a final selection one, schedule the interviews about 30 minutes apart and limit the questions to five or six. If the interviews are second-round ones, then the questions can be more specific.

You might also consider posing both oral and written questions. Begin with the oral questions and, if the committee decides that a candidate is qualified, then give the candidate several questions to answer in writing before leaving for the day. In close situations, candidates' written responses may be crucial in helping to make the final decision, because they are available for rereading and discussion. Special education teachers often must perform under pressure. Answering written questions on an impromptu basis provides valuable information about how candidates perform under pressure and how well they write.

> *The bottom line in hiring anyone is to hire the most knowledgeable, competent and cooperative person you can. The more knowledgeable, competent, and cooperative your staff, the better your program is going to be.*

Good writing skills are essential to any teacher's success. In the field of special education, poor writing skills can lead to due process hearings and professional and district embarrassment.

Asking a candidate to teach a demonstration lesson is an idea that is becoming more popular. This is a great way to see whether candidates are able to put into practice what they have talked about in the interview. Some candidates can present an excellent showcase of knowledge during the interview but cannot deliver in front of a class. Others who may not present well in an interview can be excellent teachers. Demonstration lessons are usually part of the second-round interview; to keep the process efficient, the committee only observes demonstration lessons of the top candidates.

Mentoring New Special Education Teachers

Most school districts today have some kind of mentoring program in place. Is yours designed to accommodate special education teachers? Mentoring the special education teacher is much different than mentoring a general education teacher. For one thing, your pool of veteran teachers from which to choose a mentor is much smaller. Second, the kind of paperwork and activities the special education teacher is expected to handle is very different from the general education elementary or secondary teacher's paperwork and activities. Matching the new teacher with a knowledgeable, competent, and friendly veteran is essential to a new teacher's success.

Although many districts and schools have a general informational packet that they give to all new staff (whether general or special education, elementary or secondary), there is usually a dearth of specific information for the special education teacher. There are some good reasons for this. Special education law, regulations, and case law change frequently. By the time practice and procedure catch up, it is time to change again. Keeping up with these changes is challenging, even when you are a specialist. In addition, most employees who have the responsibility of creating mentoring systems and orientation programs are not familiar with special education.

As principal, you can remedy this situation for your new special education staff. Perhaps you can work with your district's supervisor of special education to compile a special education manual (see box, "Contents of Special Education Manual"), or elicit the support of a county consultant or state educational agency personnel. Your region or state may already have developed this sort of information for new teachers. One of your special education teachers might be willing to develop information that is more specific to your school. However you create or obtain one, a special education staff manual is an absolute necessity if you wish to run an efficient and effective special education program.

Contents of Special Education Manual

- Information on school and district IEP process, from referrals for evaluation through IEP development and implementation, and information on extended school year program
- Information on governing federal and state legislation and regulations
- Report cards and progress reports
- Budgeting and purchase order forms
- Information on curricular adaptations and modifications and classroom accommodations for special education students
- Effective use of media and technology
- Student grouping, peer tutoring, and peer mentors
- Maximizing instructional time
- Lesson sequencing
- Adapting materials

Supporting New Employees[1]

How and when you observe new staff is often a matter of style. Whereas some principals believe in letting staff know when they are going to observe a classroom, others believe in the "surprise! I'm here" approach, and some operate under both provisions. Regardless of your approach to classroom observations, our first suggestion is not to do any formal observations in the first 2 months of a new teacher's placement. Even veteran teachers need time to acclimate to a new district, building, and departmental procedures; new staff, student, and parent personalities and demands; and new district, building, and departmental curricula. This is an overwhelming challenge. They do not need pressure from you at this time. It is worthwhile, however, to walk in and out of their classrooms for a few minutes at a time during those first 2 months. This lets them know you are interested in what they are doing.

Following a clinical evaluation format when observing new staff is helpful, because it provides a structure for the process: meet with the teacher before you observe, observe the teacher in the classroom, and then meet with the teacher after the observation. If you did not have candidates do a demonstration lesson as part of the hiring process, this will be your first opportunity to see the new teacher deliver a full lesson. Take advantage of this opportunity for both your own and the new teacher's benefit.

During the **pre-observation** meeting, let the teacher know what you have been observing while walking around the building and in and of the classroom; emphasize the positive. Your intent here is to set the teacher at ease and to explain what will happen next. After choosing a date and time for your formal observation, discuss exactly what you will be evaluating. Give the teacher a copy of the blank observation or evaluation form you use to record data and distill observations. There should be no surprises; this provides the teacher with a preview of both the process and its product. Before visiting the classroom, ask the teacher to provide you with a seating chart, a copy of the instructional materials or texts that will be used at the time of your observation, and a brief description of the class. The description of the class should contain information pertinent to particular students: medical issues, behavioral issues, and instructional issues. Also establish a date and time for the post-observation meeting—the more proximate to the observation date the better.

During the **observation**, make sure you see the entire cycle of a lesson: opening, middle, and closing. You want to see how well the students stay with the teacher's instruction and how many different strategies and

---

[1] We note that the information presented in this section is equally applicable to both special education teachers and general education or content-area teachers.

techniques the teacher demonstrates during the lesson (see box, "Checklist for Observing New Teachers").

Checklist for Observing New Teachers

- How did the teacher deal with classroom disruptions and discipline problems?
- How smooth were transitions from one activity to another?
- How well did the teacher sequence the lesson? Evaluate both individual lesson sequencing—opening, review, instruction, practice (individual or group)—and multiple lesson sequencing (introduction to new material, guided practice, mastery learning outcomes).
- What different types of media (chalkboard or whiteboard, computers, hands-on materials) did the teacher use?
- Did the teacher move around the room and interact with individual students?
- How did the teacher ask questions? Did questions allow for processing time?
- How well did the teacher accommodate students with physical impairments (vision, hearing, and motor)?
- What method has the teacher used for classroom arrangement?
- What method does the teacher use to group students?
- Were students on task throughout the lesson?
- Does the teacher have and did the teacher establish rapport with the students?
- Did the teacher provide effective and sufficient guided-practice materials and were these materials adapted to individual student needs?
- Did the teacher demonstrate any interesting or innovative practices to provide greater teaching/learning efficiency and effectiveness?

The **post-observation** meeting should occur in your office (this diminishes the chance for interruptions by others). After your observation, you will have a good sense of the skill level(s) of the teacher.

Begin with those things that you found positive about the lesson. If there were not many, talk about the students and their diagnosed problems or challenges, and invite the teacher to provide any insights. The post-observation meeting should be as "formative" as possible: Instead of criticizing a teacher for not doing this or that, talk about best practice and when you saw the teacher executing best practice. If there were glaring errors or omissions, save those until the end of your conversation—but do not end on a negative note. Always thank teachers for their efforts and tell them that you are ready to help them improve. Suggestions for supporting new teachers who show signs of needing improvement include:

- Consultation with the teacher's mentor;

- Consultation with a curriculum specialist, instructional coach, or a regional or county consultant;

- Sending the teacher to an inservice training; and

- Providing the teacher with resources (a book, handout, video, or web site) about a particular subject.

If you are lucky, there is someone in your district in charge of teacher development. Perhaps there already is an established development program to help support new or struggling teachers. Through training sessions and formative observation, new and almost-new teachers can improve through readings, videotapes, and live demonstrations of effective instructional practice. Bear in mind that these methods of growth and improvement are not only for teachers who need help but also for those who are interested in more general professional growth. All teachers should have a professional growth agenda, whether rookies or veterans.

> *The intent of the post-observation session is to alert teachers as needed to the particulars of the teaching model that you are using and the kinds of teaching preparation and instructional procedures that you favor.*

Professional Development of Veteran Teachers

You will probably want to take a different (i.e., gradual/sequential) approach regarding observing of and professional development planning for veteran teachers. Once you have developed staff that you consider competent in all of the basics, you might feel you can abandon the clinical model for the "drop-in" approach. By doing this, you are saying that your teachers have progressed to such an extent that—aside from the annual formal evaluation most districts require—you no longer need to evaluate their basic competency or teaching approaches, and trust that they do a good job. Therefore, you will only occasionally observe them, and informally. Ask them to invite you to their classrooms when they are doing a special activity or culminating event; this is a great opportunity for staff to be creative and to receive recognition. Also try, when possible, to publicize their accomplishments (e.g., an in-house message, district publication, or in the local press).

If your district does not already require teachers to keep a record of their professional development activities, you should initiate this in your building. This does not have to be onerous; it is a simple recordkeeping task done by each teacher during the course of the year. Every time they watch an educational video, attend an inservice training, take a mini-course or university course, read an educationally related book and implement an idea contained therein, attend a conference, or a combination of any of the above, they would mark this on their professional development log sheet. You will want to periodically review these and can reward staff who have worked hard at improving themselves by providing them with release time to participate in additional development activities, perhaps along with some professional development money to spend on these activities.

> *Your professional development program should focus on the teaching preparation and instructional procedures that you favor. You want to ensure that both new teachers and veterans are aware of best practices and innovative instructional and behavior management strategies.*

Highly Qualified Teachers

The No Child Left Behind Act of 2001 (2006) requires special education teachers to be "highly qualified" in and primary teachers of a core subject (i.e., English, math, science, social studies; 34 C.F.R. § 200.56). Although some teachers may be highly qualified in two, three, or all four core subjects, others may be highly qualified in one core subject.

A teacher's status as "highly qualified" can change from year to year—or even within a school year—based on student enrollment, transfer of a student, or an IEP change. For example, Teacher A is assigned to 22 students throughout a day, providing primary instruction in English and science to 15 students and English only to seven students in a pull-out resource environment. Teacher A, therefore, is required to be highly qualified in English and science. During the school year, a new student transfers into Teacher A's class. The student's IEP requires the student receive primary instruction in math in the resource room environment; Teacher A is now required to be highly qualified in English, science, and math.

Students who do not receive instruction from a general education teacher in a core subject and whose IEP states that instruction in that core area is required must be taught by a highly qualified special education teacher in that subject. If a student in Teacher D's self-contained class receives instruction in English only from a general education teacher and the IEP states that instruction in all core subjects should be provided, then Teacher D must be highly qualified in math, science and social studies.

As a principal, you have a dual concern: You need to both service students and meet the highly qualified teacher requirements without overburdening any one teacher. By ensuring your teachers are highly qualified in more than one subject, your students will receive more focused and specialized instruction, and you will have more flexibility in scheduling.

What Does a Principal Need to Know About Special Education Eligibility?

To receive special education services, students need to be determined to be eligible, as specified by federal law. This chapter describes the process from pre-referral through assessment. The principal's role in the process is multifaceted, ensuring that appropriate procedures and timelines are followed, while also working to meet the needs of the student in the classroom. Any problems in the procedures used in determining a child's eligibility call into question every aspect of the services provided to the student. Because the Individuals With Disabilities Education Act (IDEA, 2006) enumerates specific procedures for determining eligibility, it is very important that the principal have a thorough understanding of the law.

Quick Points

- Not all students in need of classroom supports or accommodations are eligible for special education services.

- School staff should document any pre-referral interventions and their outcomes.

- Schools need to follow timelines for responding to referrals and making decisions promptly.

- Parents or guardians need to be included at every stage of the process.

- Some students who are not be eligible for services under IDEA may be eligible under Section 504, and the evaluation process is different for each.

IDEA regulations provide specific guidelines to ensure appropriate assessment of children for special education services; the first step is to determine whether a disability exists. If, because of this disability, the student needs special education and related services, then the school needs to identify the student's specific needs and develop an individualized education program (IEP; see Chapter 4) that responds to those needs. IDEA requires that a "team of qualified professionals"—including the student's parent or guardian—determine eligibility for special education and related services (34 C.F.R. § 300.308).

For most children, the process of determining eligibility begins in the general education classroom. It may begin when the classroom teacher notices that something, either academic or behavioral, is different about this child as compared to the others. Potential problems a student may demonstrate include:

- Difficulty performing at grade level,
- Difficulty paying attention,
- Difficulty following directions,
- Difficulty getting along with others, or
- Difficulty using fine or gross motor skills.

However, not keeping pace with the rest of the class does not automatically equate to eligibility for special education. In fact, many of the problems that students exhibit in the general education classroom can and should be handled there. Perhaps what might be needed is simply to move the student closer to the board or to the teacher, or to provide the student basic assistance with organizing materials or personal space (e.g., desk, locker). Whatever problem the student exhibits, the first step is to try to ameliorate it within the general education classroom setting. This is called *pre-referral intervention*; one example of this is the response to intervention (RTI) model (see box, "Response to Intervention").

Pre-Referral Intervention

The purpose of pre-referral intervention is to find ways to increase the student's success in the general education classroom without making changes to the grade-level curriculum. Implementing pre-referral interventions and strategies also helps general education teachers develop skills and approaches that respond to the increasing variability in the learning characteristics of the students they teach. Teachers need to be able to identify a student's academic or behavioral needs; to adapt or modify materials, assignments, or the environment to respond to these needs; and to determine whether this assists the student in making progress. Pre-referral interventions can be very informal. Often simply providing universal classroom supports (e.g., guided notes, breaking down assignment into steps, visual reminders) precludes the need for special education services. However, in every case where a teacher screens a student's needs and implements pre-referral interventions, data on the success or failure of the interventions must be collected. This data will help determine whether further interventions are needed. If the data demonstrate that the student is now successful, further interventions are not needed and the student continues in the general education curriculum. If the data suggest that further interventions are needed, then the referral process begins.

Response to Intervention

According to IDEA, a student cannot be determined to have a disability if the determining factor is that the student has not received scientifically based instructional practices and programs that contain the essential components of reading instruction, has not received appropriate instruction in math, or has limited English proficiency (34 CFR § 300.306[b][1]). In addition, rather than only looking at a discrepancy between achievement and intellectual ability, the local educational agency (i.e., someone at the child's school) can use a process that determines if a child responds to scientific, research-based intervention. This model has been labeled *response to intervention* (RTI). In the RTI process, evaluation and intervention essentially are conducted concurrently. Proponents of the RTI model contend that this approach avoids the traditional discrepancy model's problem of "waiting for the child to fail." In addition, the discrepancy approach does not incorporate intervention, and there can be both false positives and false negatives with IQ and achievement testing.

The RTI model has at its basis a three-tier decision-making process (a model derived from community mental health service) that has primarily been applied to reading instruction. In this model, Tier 1 is screening and schoolwide intervention; for example, an early literacy program that has both an instructional and a screening component is applied to all students. Tier 2 is assessing response to this instruction during team-based problem solving. Tier 3 is appraising the extent of academic problems and evaluating the need for specially designed instruction (i.e., the traditional model of special education services).

RTI can identify students who have not been making expected progress in the general education curriculum and are considered to be at risk for academic failure; for example, a student who is not learning to read in kindergarten would be considered not to be making progress. Once a student had been identified as being at risk, long- and short-term goals are set for that student's progress to establish benchmarks and standards. The student's progress is then monitored in reference to the established goals and benchmarks. Academic interventions are adjusted frequently in relation to monitoring the child's performance.

The principal often never hears about the students for whom teachers successfully modify instruction because the basic modifications worked and there is no need for additional follow-up. There are some students, however, whose needs are more complex: Although the teacher has worked to modify instruction, tried different teaching strategies, and provided basic classroom supports, there is no discernible difference in the student's academic progress. The principal often hears about these students (especially if they also exhibit behavior problems).

Most states have specific procedures for pre-referral intervention and these vary; however, it is important to note that this may be only the first step in providing assistance to a student. If more intensive interventions than those defined in the pre-referral process are needed, you should seek parent permission and conduct an evaluation.

During the pre-referral process teachers should document everything that demonstrates the extent of the student's difficulties and any attempts that have been made to effect change. Even if the teacher has notified the principal of the problem, it is necessary to go beyond discussion to documentation. The teacher should collect examples of the student's work compared to others in the class. As appropriate, teachers may need to provide examples of behavior and when and where it is demonstrated, or time samples of off-task behavior. This is where it may be important for you, your school counselor, or your school psychologist to offer assistance by observing the student in the classroom and making recommendations. With a detailed description of the problem from the teacher, an observation by another professional may help to further define the problem or assist in identifying instructional or behavioral strategies to ameliorate the student's difficulties.

The use of pre-referral interventions cannot deny the services that a student may need by delaying the assessment process.

For these observations, it can be helpful to use a systematic observation system such as Shapiro's Behavioral Observation of Students in Schools (BOSS; 2010) or the Behavior Assessment for Children's (BASC-2; Reynolds & Kamphaus, 2004) Student Observation System. Both of these systematic behavioral rating systems allow comparison of the behavior of the target student with a peer match. Why is it important to compare the student to another student in the class? Suppose that a teacher reports a student as being off task 50% of the time. This might seem like an important piece of information and might indicate that the student is having problems. However, if other students in the class are only on task 30% to 40% of the time, the student who is on task 50% is doing pretty well.

Referral for Special Education Evaluation

A referral to determine if special education services are necessary should be initiated if a student still does not make progress even after the teacher has tried different interventions. Teachers, educational specialists, school counselors, administrators, and parents can initiate referrals. It is important to emphasize that the pre-referral process of working to improve the child's performance should not delay a referral (34 C.F.R. §§ 300.304–300.311). When there is a referral, even if you are working to implement pre-referral interventions, the decision about whether testing is necessary must be made within 10 days. If a student's parents or guardians request testing and the team decides testing is not necessary, the parents need to be notified in writing. At that time, they also need to be notified of their due process rights. A *referral* is a request for testing and should document the reasons why the child should be assessed for special education eligibility. It should give some indication of the problem areas of the student. Most districts have formal referral forms (see sample, Figure 3.1).

Parents who initiate a referral do not need to provide the same supporting documentation requested of teachers; they just need to put in writing that they want their child tested. As a principal and a member of the multidisciplinary team, you can gather the information from the other members of the team to determine if testing is warranted.

Initial Multidisciplinary Team Meeting

After a referral is received, the initial multidisciplinary team meeting is held to determine if the child warrants testing. Under IDEA regulations, the team can choose not to evaluate a child if they feel there is no basis to suspect that there is a disability. For example, psychological evaluations may not be appropriate if the student is not having any academic issues at school and does not demonstrate behaviors suggesting psychological difficulties.

The multidisciplinary team should include a general education teacher, an individual knowledgeable of the suspected disability, the parent(s) or guardian(s), and an administrator (frequently, the principal). As principal, it is appropriate for you to participate on the team; as discussed in the Introduction, you should make it a practice to know the students in your school (particularly those who are struggling), and should be able to recognize how this particular student is functioning compared to other students in the building.

Prior to the meeting, certain information will need to be collected, such as examples of class work from the student and grade-level peers (for comparison), notes from any observations of the student, results from screening instruments

Figure 3.1
Sample Referral for Special Education Evaluation

Student name:	
Address:	Grade: Birth date:
Tel. #	Teacher/counselor:
Person who made referral:	Date referral initiated:
Relationship:	

Reason for referral (please specify)

    Instructional concerns:

    Behavioral concerns:

Pre-referral interventions: (Describe any current or past supplemental programs/services or interventions provided to the child. Describe any scientific research-based interventions implemented and the results.)

or normative tests, report cards and reports from previous teachers, and comments from other staff who interact with the student (e.g., art teacher, PE teacher). You will also want to include any behavioral reports on the student, in addition to academic records.

It is essential that the meeting follow an organized process; Figure 3.2 provides a sample agenda with discussion items and questions designed to cover all essential concerns and information. Ensure that one member of the team is assigned to take notes during the meeting and keep track of any documentation.

Following the meeting, make sure the notes or minutes describe what occurred with the specific recommendations. Forward a written copy of the results of the meeting to the parents, the child's permanent file, and the

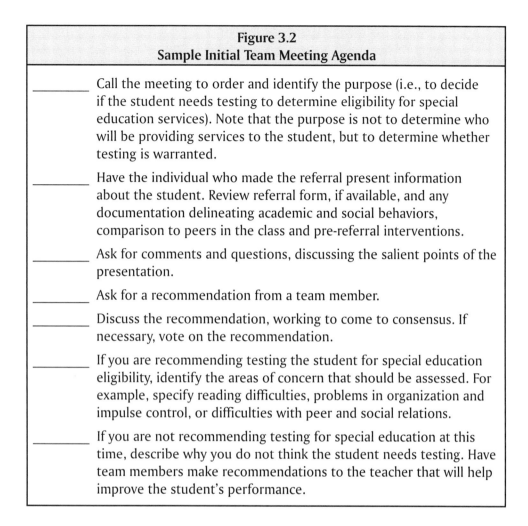

Figure 3.2
Sample Initial Team Meeting Agenda

_____ Call the meeting to order and identify the purpose (i.e., to decide if the student needs testing to determine eligibility for special education services). Note that the purpose is not to determine who will be providing services to the student, but to determine whether testing is warranted.

_____ Have the individual who made the referral present information about the student. Review referral form, if available, and any documentation delineating academic and social behaviors, comparison to peers in the class and pre-referral interventions.

_____ Ask for comments and questions, discussing the salient points of the presentation.

_____ Ask for a recommendation from a team member.

_____ Discuss the recommendation, working to come to consensus. If necessary, vote on the recommendation.

_____ If you are recommending testing the student for special education eligibility, identify the areas of concern that should be assessed. For example, specify reading difficulties, problems in organization and impulse control, or difficulties with peer and social relations.

_____ If you are not recommending testing for special education at this time, describe why you do not think the student needs testing. Have team members make recommendations to the teacher that will help improve the student's performance.

individual in your district responsible for coordinating testing. The letter needs to have the child's name, birth date, current grade placement, teacher's name, and school. In addition, it should include your recommendation as to whether the child should be tested or not and any recommendations for specific areas of assessment. Finally, it should include the team member's names and signatures. If the parents made the referral for testing and you are making the recommendation that the child not be tested, then a copy of the due process rights need to be included in the letter mailed to the parent.

Evaluation for Special Education Eligibility

If the multidisciplinary team recommends testing the student to determine eligibility for special education, the next step is to obtain parental consent. This means that:

- Parents must be notified in writing of intent to assess a student for special education eligibility and the reasons for the assessment, and must be provided with a written statement of their rights under the law. This statement needs to be understandable to the public.

- Parents need to be apprised of their due process rights. They also need an explanation of the tests, who will be doing the testing, when the tests will occur, and how long the process will take.

- Parents need to be aware of what the likely results would be if the child is found eligible for special education.

- Parents need to acknowledge they have received their notice of rights.

For testing to occur, the parents need to provide consent. If the parents do not provide consent for an evaluation, or the parent fails to respond to a request to provide consent, due process hearing procedures may be used to obtain authority for the evaluation.

Federal regulations are very prescriptive about evaluating students for special education services (34 C.F.R. § 300.304; see Table 3.1). It is important for principals to understand the procedures so that they can help monitor the process, and help answer questions about the appropriateness or the stage of the process.

All students suspected of eligibility for special education services receive tests in general intelligence, vision, hearing, and academic performance. The selection of other tests should be based on recommendations from the initial multidisciplinary team. If the team suspects a reading problem, for example, there should be additional assessments in reading. The assessment process for the student needs to be individualized, based on the referral. A standardized assessment provided to every child suspected of having a disability violates the spirit of the law, and does not serve to assess what the specific child might need. Individualization also means that a group-administered test may be used to "screen" for a disability, but not for a disability determination.

The National Association of School Psychologists (NASP) describes psychological evaluations as a "set of assessment procedures administered by a licensed psychologist or credentialed school psychologist to obtain information about a student's learning, behavior, or mental health" (Canter, 2003). Psychologists use different assessment procedures or combinations of procedures—standardized tests, rating scales, self-report measures, observation, and interviews—depending the reason for the evaluation (Canter, 2003):

> *Evaluations may also be conducted to develop behavioral and instructional interventions, identify metal health disorders, and identify giftedness and school readiness.*

Table 3.1 Evaluating Students for Special Education Eligibility	
General principles	No single procedure is to be used as the sole criterion for determining whether a child is a child with a disability and for determining an appropriate educational program for the child.
	The child is to be assessed in all areas related to the suspected disability including, if appropriate, health, vision, hearing, social and emotional status, general intelligence, academic performance, communicative status, and motor abilities.
	In evaluating each child with a disability, the evaluation is to be sufficiently comprehensive as to identify all of the child's special education and related services needs, whether or not commonly linked to the disability category in which the child has been classified.
	Technically sound instruments are to be used that may assess the relative contribution of cognitive and behavioral factors, in addition to physical or developmental factors.
	Assessment tools and strategies must be used that provide relevant information that directly assists persons in determining the educational needs of the child.
Assessment devices or tests	Tests are selected and administered so as not to be discriminatory on a racial or cultural basis.
	Tests are provided and administered in the child's native language or other mode of communication, unless it is clearly not feasible to do so.
	Tests used to assess a child with limited English proficiency are to be selected to ensure they measure the extent to which the child has a disability and needs special education, rather than measuring the child's English language skills.
	A variety of assessment tools and strategies are used to gather relevant functional and developmental information about the child, including information provided by the parent, and information related to enabling the child to be involved in and progress in the general curriculum (or for a preschool child, to participate in appropriate activities), that may assist in determining whether the child is a child with a disability.

Table 3.1 *(continued)* Evaluating Students for Special Education Eligibility	
Standardized tests	Standardized tests must have been validated for the specific purpose for which they are used.
	Standardized tests are to be administered by trained and knowledgeable personnel in accordance with any instructions provided by the producer of the tests.
	If an assessment is not conducted under standard conditions, a description of the extent to which it varied from standard conditions (e.g., the qualifications of the person administering the test, or the method of test administration) must be included in the evaluation report.
	Tests and other evaluation materials must be tailored to assess specific areas of educational need and not merely designed to provide a single general intelligence quotient.
	Tests must be selected to ensure that if a test is administered to a child with impaired sensory, manual, or speaking skills, the results accurately reflect the child's aptitude or achievement level or whatever other factors the test purports to measure, rather than reflecting the child's impaired sensory, manual, or speaking skills (unless those skills are the factors that the test purports to measure).

- **Standardized (normed) tests** enable a comparison of a student's performance to an appropriate peer group. Three common standards of intelligence testing are the Wechsler Intelligence Scale for Children (WISC; Wechsler, 2004), the Stanford-Binet (Roid, 2003), and the Woodcock Johnson Test of Cognitive Abilities (Woodcock, Mather, & McGrew, 2001).

- **Rating scales** assess "the presence or frequency of certain behaviors or skills" (Canter, 2003) and are usually completed by parents and teachers. Rating scales are also normed to particular populations to help highlight behaviors that are significantly different from peers. Rating scales can be "broad band" measures like the BASC-2 (Reynolds & Kamphaus, 2004), or they can be behavior specific; for example, the Conners Rating Scale (2008) is specifically geared for diagnosis of ADHD.

- School-aged children can complete **self-report measures** that provide insight into their internal state and may help identify specific conditions or disorders (e.g., the Beck Depression Inventory; Beck, 1996).

- **Observations** give an indication of how the student functions in the academic environment and interactions with others. For example, observing students in unstructured periods of the day (e.g., recess, lunch, transitions), can be very helpful in identifying characteristics of autism spectrum disorder.

- **Interviewing** students can help in the gathering of information regarding: interpersonal relationships, history, and prominent concerns. Similarly, interviewing parents and teachers allows one to gather critical information regarding medical, developmental, and educational history.

It is important to emphasize that the assessment must include all areas related to the suspected disability and be comprehensive enough to identify all required special education and related services needs. The time from when parents give consent for testing to the time that a meeting is held to determine whether a child is eligible for special education is prescribed by federal and state law. IDEA specifies a 60-day timeline from receipt of parent consent to completion of the evaluation (34 C.F.R. § 300.301[c]).

The members of the multidisciplinary team conduct the evaluation. Additional members (e.g., physicians, nurses, school psychologists) may be added after the initial meeting. At least one member of the team must be knowledgeable about the suspected disability. For example, if you suspect the student has a learning disability, one member of the team must be qualified to teach students with learning disabilities. Any team member who conducts an observation or administers a test or assessment must be qualified to do so.

Evaluation for Related Services

As discussed in Chapter 1, students who need special education often need related services in order for them to receive the benefits of education. If, based upon the initial referral, you suspect a student may need related services, then the student needs to be evaluated for such services by individuals trained in the appropriate techniques. For example, if you are assessing a child for services on the basis of intellectual disability but suspect there may also be a need for physical therapy, then an individual trained in providing assessments in physical therapy needs to assess the child. All assessments for related services (e.g., occupational therapy, speech and language services, counseling services) have to occur within the same period as the other assessments.

After gathering the information from the assessments, the multidisciplinary team needs to meet to review the results. Because principals often lead these types of team meetings, it is important for you to understand the different members' roles, the information expected from them, and the result of the meeting. Figure 3.3 provides a checklist of steps to follow when scheduling and conducting a multidisciplinary team meeting to evaluate students for special education support.

Figure 3.3 Checklist for Multidisciplinary Team Meeting	
Scheduling the meeting	
	Schedule the meeting within the specified times as delineated by your state. Generally, any meeting should occur within 60 days after the signed approval of the parents.
	Ensure all participants will be able to attend (e.g., person making referral, administrators of testing or assessments, general education teacher, someone knowledgeable of suspected disability).
	Schedule the meeting at a time that is convenient to the parent(s) or guardian(s).
	Arrange to hold the meeting in a comfortable, quiet, and distraction-free room. Plan to meet for about 2 hours.
	If holding the meeting during the school day, arrange for substitute teachers for educators attending the meeting.
Before the meeting	
	Collect the results of all tests or assessments, and summaries of the results. Discuss the results with those who conducted the assessments to ensure no additional testing is necessary. (If it appears that additional testing is required, conduct this before the meeting as well.)
	Ensure that all participants know the date, time, purpose, and location of the meeting.
	Ensure that all participants can attend. If one of the members is unable to attend, decide whether to reschedule (within the confines of your state's timelines) or whether to present a summary of the individual's input at the meeting. Identify who will present the summary.
	Identify a note taker for the meeting.
	Ensure that office staff know that some attendees may not be familiar with the school (they may need to direct them to the correct location), and that they understand the importance of the meeting and that it is not to be interrupted.
	Ensure that the parent(s) or guardian(s) receive a copy of the evaluation in advance. (Most states have specific guidelines about this; 10 days in advance is a good timeframe.)

	Figure 3.3 (continued) **Checklist for Multidisciplinary Team Meeting**
	Conducting the meeting
	Open the meeting by welcoming all participants and explaining the purpose (i.e., to review assessment information to determine if the student is eligible for special education services).
	Ask all participants to introduce themselves; for school/district employees, have them explain or describe their professional role.
	Stress that all information presented and discussed at the meeting is confidential.
	Have all participants sign an attendance sheet and indicate their names and titles/relationship to student.
	Explain that everyone will have an opportunity to ask questions after each report. Explain or provide a list of any acronyms or abbreviations used in the reports.
	Explain that after the presentation and discussion of all reports, the team will make a decision about whether the child is eligible for special education services. Note that the meeting is not to recommend course selections or identify teaching personnel.
	Have the person who initiated the referral state the problems the student was having and why the referral was made.
	Have any participants who conducted observations or administered tests or assessments present the results of their activities. *All participants should describe the child accurately, and note strengths as well as challenges; this is a child who may need support, not just numbers in a manila folder. The reason for the meeting is to improve the child's educational experience.*
	After each report has been presented, ask for comments or questions.
	Review the definition of the suspected disability. *You may need to read more than one definition (e.g., when unsure whether a child who is demonstrating behavior problems has a learning disability or an emotional and behavioral disorder).*
	Based on the definition(s) as read, ask for a recommendation as to whether the child qualifies for special education services.
	Discuss the recommendation and respond to any questions relating to the definition(s).
	Ask for a show of hands or other indication of being for or against the recommendation.

	Figure 3.3 *(continued)* **Checklist for Multidisciplinary Team Meeting**	
	Conducting the meeting *(continued)*	
	Summarize the recommendation(s), ensuring that the note taker's report is accurate. *If any team members are opposed to the recommendation, note that they may file a minority report.*
	Ask the parents if they have any questions about the process, and note that they have the right to file a due process at any time if they are unhappy with the outcome of the meeting or the educational services provided to the student.
	Thank all participants for their attendance and their contributions. Adjourn the meeting.
	After the meeting	
	As soon as possible, review the notes to make sure they accurately reflect what occurred.
	If the child is eligible for special education services, make sure the director of special education or director of pupil personnel services is aware; provide this individual with a copy of the meeting notes.
	Place a copy of the meeting notes in the child's permanent file.
	If the child is eligible for special education services, the process to develop an IEP must be completed within 10 days of this decision.
	If the child is not eligible for special education services, meet with the general education teacher and additional staff members as necessary to identify strategies that might support the student.
	Be available to meet with the parent or guardian to review the meeting. *If you are not immediately able to answer all questions, find the answers rather than referring them to others.*
	Note. See Appendix C for a list of commonly used education abbreviations and acronyms.

There are different recommendations that the team can make: that the child is eligible for special education, that the child is not eligible for special education, or that the decision be deferred because additional information is necessary or because some major life event occurred necessitating a waiting period (e.g., mother is very sick). If deferring the decision, the team needs to document the reason for the wait, obtain approval from the parent(s), and set a specific deadline for reconvening the meeting. This waiting period should be brief, for a specific function, and should not be used to delay services. Regardless of the decision reached by the multidisciplinary team, the parent or guardian must receive a written report summarizing the findings from the meeting, recommendations for ways of improving service, test scores and summaries, and notes from observations.

Because the information in a student's IEP stems directly from the comprehensive evaluation report, if the child is determined to be eligible for special education services, the comprehensive evaluation report also should specify the disability and describe the child's strengths and weaknesses, list the broad goals toward which the child should be working, and include a minority report if there was not unanimity.

Triennial Evaluation

Students who receive special education services under IDEA must be reevaluated at least once every 3 years. The intent of reevaluation is to determine if the student is still eligible and still requires special education support, and, if so, that the services provided match the student's needs. The big difference between the initial evaluation and the triennial or reevaluation is that the child does not have to go through the same complete battery of tests as the first time. As long as the reevaluation addresses the student's current needs, it does not have to be identical. The reevaluation, however, should be similar to the original placement evaluation.

The term *triennial* describes the need for the evaluation to occur at least once every 3 years. If the student is making progress or the program does not seem to fit based on the previous evaluation, then it is entirely appropriate to conduct evaluations more frequently.

Evaluation for Section 504 Accommodation

There are subtle differences in the evaluation procedures of Section 504 and those of IDEA. It is important for principals to have a thorough understanding of these differences, because in many districts the principal is the one responsible for ensuring that students with disabilities are having their needs met under Section 504 (Madaus & Shaw, 2008).

As with assessing students for special education eligibility under IDEA, when evaluating whether students require Section 504 accommodations, there are governing federal regulations and directives to "ensure that children are not misclassified, unnecessarily labeled as having a disability, or incorrectly placed, based on inappropriate selection, administration, or interpretation of evaluation materials" (Office of Civil Rights, 2009). To this end, schools need to ensure that:

(1) Tests and all evaluation materials have been validated for the specific purpose for which they are used and are administered by trained personnel in conformity with instructions provided by their producer;

(2) Tests and other evaluation materials include those tailored to assess specific areas of educational need and not merely those which are designed to provide a single intelligence quotient; and

(3) Tests are selected and administered so as to best ensure that, when a test is administered to a student with impaired sensory, manual, or speaking skill, the test results accurately reflect the student's aptitude or achievement level or whatever other factor the test purports to measure, rather than reflecting the student's impaired [abilities] (except when those skills are the factors that the test purports to measure). (34 C.F.R. § 104.35[b])

When evaluating a student for Section 504 accommodations a school must convene a group of persons knowledgeable about the student who understand the data from the tests and can make appropriate decisions about placement. As with IDEA, the school must notify parents of their rights to file a grievance, to be notified when eligibility is determined, to an evaluation that uses multiple sources, to periodic reevaluation, and to representation by counsel when needed.

Independent Education Evaluation

If the parents do not feel the evaluation of their child is adequate, they can request an independent educational evaluation (IEE) at public expense. A qualified individual not affiliated with the district conducts the IEE. The IEE can cover the same territory as the school's evaluation, or it can cover only part, such as diagnostic information about reading or a different intelligence test.

When a parent requests an IEE, the school should be prepared to provide a list of qualified individuals who administer such evaluations. The school must consider the results of the IEE as a part of its decision making, though it does not have to accept the results as the definitive statement of the child's educational performance. If the school does not accept the results of the IEE, it must provide the parents in writing with a description of how the independent evaluation was made available to the district, a record of the subsequent discussion, and reasons for the disagreement.

> *Parents can request an independent educational evaluation at any time in the process.*

A district does not have to grant a parent's request for an IEE at public expense if it believes the original evaluation is appropriate. If the parents disagree with the district about whether the evaluation was appropriate, however, they have the right to call for a due process hearing. If a due process hearing officer deems an IEE is necessary, then the district should arrange for an independent evaluation as soon as possible. In the event the due process hearing officer does not state an IEE is necessary, the parents still have the right to obtain one at their own expense. In fact, families may obtain as many IEEs at their expense as they want. The process for reviewing information when a parent pays for an IEE is the same as when the district pays for the evaluation: The team needs to meet regarding the results, consider them, and, if not using the results, it should state why.

A final note on IEEs: the ultimate goal in obtaining an evaluation of a child is to assist in planning appropriate instruction. Consider any request for an IEE very carefully, keeping in mind the rationale behind the request. When results from any evaluation are presented—regardless of who conducted the assessments—review them in light of how to improve the education of the child.

Disability Categories

For students to receive special education services under IDEA, they must meet at least one of the 13 categorical definitions (see Appendix B). Your state may have a different definition than the ones the federal government uses; however, these serve as at least a benchmark from which to compare. These are the definitions used as a part of the multidisciplinary team decision.

Attention Deficit Hyperactivity Disorder

Students with ADHD may receive special education services and classroom support, accommodations, or modifications, either under IDEA or Section 504. IDEA includes ADHD among the "acute health problems" that may qualify a student for services under the Other Health Impairment category. To be eligible for special education services under IDEA, students with ADHD have to demonstrate "limited strength, vitality, or alertness, including a heightened alertness to environmental stimuli, that results in limited alertness with respect to the educational environment, that ... adversely affects ... educational performance" (34 C.F.R. § 300.8[c][9]).

For students with ADHD to be eligible for Section 504 accommodations, the school must determine that the student's ADHD "substantially limits one or more" major life activities, which include "caring for one's self, performing manual tasks, walking, seeing, hearing, speaking, breathing, learning, and working" (34 C.F.R. § 104.3).

Table 3.2
Guidelines for Determining the Existence of a Specific Learning Disability

The multidisciplinary team may determine that a child has a specific learning disability, if …

The child does not achieve adequately for the child's age or to meet State-approved grade-level standards in one or more of the following areas, when provided with learning experiences and instruction appropriate for the child's age or State-approved grade-level standards: • Oral expression. • Listening comprehension. • Written expression. • Basic reading skill. • Reading fluency skills. • Reading comprehension. • Mathematics calculation. • Mathematics problem solving.	The child does not make sufficient progress to meet age or State-approved grade-level standards in one or more of these areas when using a process based on the child's response to scientific, research-based intervention; *or* The child exhibits a pattern of strengths and weaknesses in performance, achievement, or both, relative to age, State-approved grade-level standards, or intellectual development, that is determined by the group to be relevant to the identification of a specific learning disability, using appropriate assessments.	The group determines that its findings are not primarily the result of— • A visual, hearing, or motor disability; • Intellectual disability; • Emotional disturbance; • Cultural factors; • Environmental or economic disadvantage; or • Limited English proficiency.

In addition, the team must establish that the student received appropriate instruction in general education settings, and that the school assessed the student at reasonable intervals and provided the results of such assessment to the student's parent or guardian.

Note. See 34 C.F.R. § 300.309.

Learning Disabilities

Students with learning disabilities represent the largest category of those receiving services under IDEA. For this reason, it is essential that principals understand and are familiar with the guidelines for determining eligibility for the category of specific learning disability (see Table 3.2).

When a child is identified as having a specific learning disability, the team needs to produce a written report that documents the basis for making this determination. This should include the relevant behavior noted during observations and the relationship of that behavior to the child's academic functioning. In particular, the team needs to address

> whether the child does not achieve adequately for the child's age or to meet State-approved grade-level standards ... or the child exhibits a pattern of strengths and weaknesses in performance, achievement, or both, relative to age, State-approved grade level standards or intellectual development ... or the child exhibits a pattern of strengths and weaknesses in performance, achievement, or both, relative to age, State-approved grade-level standards or intellectual development. (34 C.F.R. § 300.311[a])

The team also needs to note its consideration of "the effects of a visual, hearing, or motor disability; mental retardation; emotional disturbance; cultural factors; environmental or economic disadvantage; or limited English proficiency on the child's achievement level" (34 C.F.R. § 300.311[a]) and verify that the school assessed the student's response to research-based interventions (e.g., RTI)—and reported the results of such assessment to the parents.

Quick Review

A well-developed evaluation plan is the backbone of any program for a student with a disability. Without understanding the student's functioning level, planning and providing appropriate educational services is virtually impossible. Make sure that both staff and students' families are aware of the needs of a well-developed evaluation plan.

What Is an IEP and What Is the Principal's Role?

This chapter discusses the important components of the individualized education program (IEP). Appendix E's IEP Checklists supplement information in this chapter regarding what to do before, during, and after an IEP meeting; content considerations; and can support monitoring of an individual school's process. Although IDEA does not require principals to participate on IEP teams, the IEP team must include a representative of the local education agency (LEA; i.e., school district or school) who has the authority to commit funds—so, for this reason, principals often do participate on IEP teams. It is essential for all principals to understand the IEP process, and to make sure that the individuals responsible for the development and implementation of a student's IEP have the necessary support.

Quick Points

- Know the parts of an IEP.
- Ensure the developers of the IEP have the necessary information.
- Ensure the developers of the IEP have enough time.
- Ensure that parents or guardians are notified in a timely fashion and strongly encouraged to participate.
- Ensure the IEP is implemented in a timely fashion.
- Ensure the necessary services and supports delineated in the IEP are provided.
- Ensure the IEP is evaluated at least annually.

The IEP is the most important document existing for a student with a disability. For all practical purposes, view the IEP as a contract between the district and the student's parents or guardians; courts have held in the past that failure to properly develop and implement an IEP can invalidate a program. A district that developed an IEP stating the student was to receive 90 minutes of language arts instruction five times a week, and ended up only providing three sessions a week with each lasting only 30 minutes, would be in violation of the law. It is important not only to develop an appropriate IEP for a student, but also to make sure it is being implemented. The IEP formalizes a student's education, listing the educational and intervention services to be provided, and serves many purposes: instructional, communication, management, accountability, monitoring, and evaluation (see Figure 4.1).

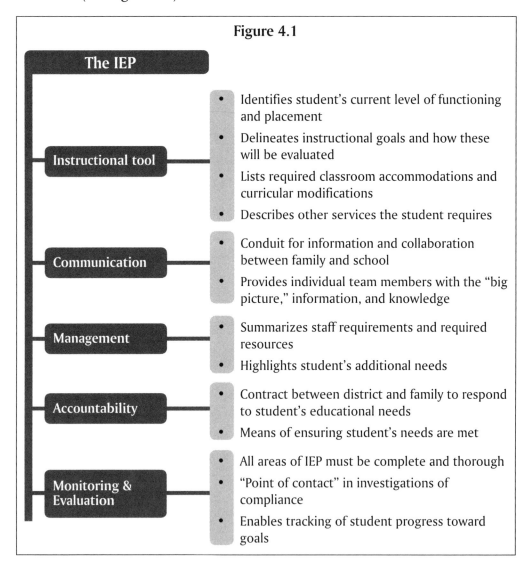

Figure 4.1

The IEP

Instructional tool
- Identifies student's current level of functioning and placement
- Delineates instructional goals and how these will be evaluated
- Lists required classroom accommodations and curricular modifications
- Describes other services the student requires

Communication
- Conduit for information and collaboration between family and school
- Provides individual team members with the "big picture," information, and knowledge

Management
- Summarizes staff requirements and required resources
- Highlights student's additional needs

Accountability
- Contract between district and family to respond to student's educational needs
- Means of ensuring student's needs are met

Monitoring & Evaluation
- All areas of IEP must be complete and thorough
- "Point of contact" in investigations of compliance
- Enables tracking of student progress toward goals

As an **instructional tool**, the IEP delineates the services provided to the student. It should be clear enough that a student can transfer between districts with the new teacher(s) picking up the IEP and knowing exactly what is required.

The IEP also serves an important **communication** function, keeping all the individuals who are a part of the student's educational experience (and, hence, part of the student's IEP team) informed about the services the student is receiving and ensuring that this is a collaborative effort (see Developing an IEP). It provides all team members with information that will assist them on a day-to-day basis. For general education teachers, it has the added benefit of enhancing understanding of the many facets of special education; for parents, it delineates the educational interventions and services provided to their child.

As a **management** device, the IEP is a reference document describing which professionals are providing services to this child and for how long each day. Because it summarizes all of a student's needs (e.g., including special counseling, transportation, paraprofessional support), the IEP provides valuable information to principals when allocating staff.

The IEP serves as a contract between the district and the parents and as such provides a means of **accountability**; by completing the IEP the district has contracted to commit resources to the student. For example, if it is stated in the IEP that a student is to receive 2 hours of instruction five times a week from a special education teacher, the student must receive 2 hours a day of instruction from a special education teacher. This does not mean instruction provided solely or mostly by an instructional aide, or 1 hour of instruction a day from a special educator; that is not what the IEP states. Note that accountability does not mean that a district may be held liable for a student not meeting the goals of the IEP. That is not what the law implies, and should not be inferred. An appropriate IEP is one in which the district has made a "good faith" effort to implement the IEP, kept track of its efforts, and, when problems occurred, worked to change it. (If, however, the district does not make a "good faith" effort to implement the IEP or respond to problems or parental concerns, then the IEP is inappropriate.)

A student's IEP can be changed to reflect changing needs.

The IEP is the "point of contact" when outside agencies or compliance officers from state boards of education investigate whether students with disabilities are being provided a free appropriate public education. Because of the IEP's role as a **monitoring** device, principals need to learn the components of the IEP and ensure all services are appropriately delineated in the document, for each individual student.

IEP goals provide guidance to schools in assessing whether a student is making progress and thus the IEP has an **evaluation** purpose, too. This is an important point to keep in mind when initially developing the IEP and, later, during the annual review and triennial reevaluation. Writing goals and objectives that include specific behavioral and academic benchmarks will help clarify whether students have achieved IEP goals. If the IEP states certain goals will be addressed by a certain date, and progress is not forthcoming, this may prompt discussion about whether the IEP needs to be revised.

Developing an IEP

The IEP is developed by a team, which includes all those relevant to a student's education: parents or guardians, general and special education teachers, counselors, related services providers, and so on (see box, "Who Should Attend an IEP Meeting?"). There are specific activities principals can do before, during, and after the IEP meeting that will make the process more efficient and ensure that the school is complying with federal regulations and guidelines. Appendix E provides additional information and guidance for activities to undertake before, during, and after an IEP is developed for a student.

Who Should Attend an IEP Meeting?

- General education teacher
- Special education teacher
- A representative of the local education agency
- Parent or guardian
- Others knowledgeable of the child and/or the disability
- Others designated by the student's family
- The student, when appropriate, especially after age 16

Before the Meeting

Everyone who participates in the IEP meeting should have a good understanding of the individual student's needs and some ideas about what the IEP should include. Although in many schools the director of special education asks and responds to questions about the student's individual needs, increasingly it is the principal who schedules, assists in or directs IEP development, and signs off as representative of the LEA. Even if you have assigned a principal designee to run the meeting, it is essential for you as principal to understand the needs of students with disabilities who attend your school and to ensure that you have amassed the resources required to meet these needs. Table 4.1 provides a checklist of things principals should do when preparing for an IEP meeting. These preparation points might seem long and involved, but the meetings themselves as a part of the information gathering process do not have to be long, and these items do not have to be accomplished in a particular sequence. Many principals "meet" with teachers as they are walking down the hall, standing in the lunchroom, and so on. The important thing is to keep these priorities in mind as you are preparing for the meeting itself.

Some districts assign an individual to develop a draft of the IEP before the meeting. The individual assigned to do this should be one who is familiar with the student, has knowledge about the student's disability, and who is experienced in writing IEPs. If your district follows this procedure, the emphasis should be on the word draft. Development of draft sections of some components of the IEP is a time-saving practice. However, it is not the final process. During the IEP meeting, stress that this is only a draft. You can make additions, delete or reword passages, or rewrite the whole document. Ensure that all participants in the meeting understand that this can be done.

Table 4.1 Preparing for the IEP Meeting	
Review the information from the multidisciplinary team's evaluation meeting (see Chapter 3)	Reviewing the referral for testing and historical records relating to the student's performance and challenges in the classroom will give you a general idea of strengths and weaknesses. The evaluation report should enhance this understanding; note that the student's strengths and weaknesses should establish the basis for the development of the IEP.
	Talk to individuals who were a part of the multidisciplinary team about their impressions of the education this student should receive. Ask them about any parts of the multidisciplinary team report that either you do not understand or with which you need clarification.
Review any previous IEPs	Specifically, look at the goals listed on previous IEPs. Compare them with the results of the evaluation report. If possible, talk with the teachers who implemented previous IEPs, and ask them for suggestions about what worked, what did not work, and what might be done differently.

Table 4.1 (continued) Preparing for the IEP Meeting	
Meet with relevant team members and school staff	Although assigning responsibility for aspects of the student's IEP will be a decision made at the meeting, talk to different members to get an idea of recommendations that might be offered for the particular student's education program. Identify the general education or content-area teachers most likely to be involved in the education of this student.
	Talk with current and past teachers about what has worked with this student, and where there have been problems. Knowing this information will provide you with valuable insight into the educational programming the student should receive.
Consider staffing requirements and resources	For the different teachers or related services personnel who might be involved with this student, look at the caseload or numbers of students for which they are responsible. State departments of education have strict guidelines about the class sizes in special education classrooms. Although it might not be your responsibility to monitor this number, you may need to bring it to the attention of others if the numbers are too high.
	If you are the least bit unsure about your school's ability to provide potential interventions, programs, technology tools, or other supports, seek clarification from your supervisor.

Table 4.1 (continued) Preparing for the IEP Meeting	
Schedule the meeting	Identify a time convenient to the student's parent or guardian, and do your best to get them involved, even if it takes several telephone calls, e-mails, or notices sent home. The IEP is a form of communication between the school and the student's family; your responsibility as principal is to ensure your school makes every effort to include them in the process. (And, for your own protection, you should document your efforts to do so.) • Make sure the parents are aware they have the right to invite to the meeting someone they view as knowledgeable about their child's disability to provide assistance in the development of the IEP (34 C.F.R. § 300.344[a][6]). • As necessary, arrange for an interpreter for parents who use sign language, or for those whose preferred language is not English; ensure that the meeting is accessible to any adult with a disability.
	The meeting should also be convenient for the special education teacher most likely to be implementing or overseeing the plan. The types of decisions that are made at IEP meetings are those that cannot be done in the classroom and with limited time. Identify as this point person someone who is a good "fit" for the student's needs, and who has the time and the caseload that permits participation. Make it easier for teachers to participate by arranging to cover their classes.
	Students participate in any IEP meetings that relate to their postsecondary transition goals; for these students, ensure that the meeting is scheduled at a time that is convenient for them, too.

Table 4.1 *(continued)* Preparing for the IEP Meeting	
Conduct student observations	Observe students in the classroom setting and other areas of the school. Note the academic behavior, social behavior, and how they handle frustration. Observe interactions with other students, how students seek assistance from others, and how well organized they appear.
	Encourage others—those who are knowledgeable about the student's disability or those who will be involved in implementing the IEP—to observe the student as well. Although, they will get to know the student after the IEP meeting, this will help them in participating in the development of the IEP.

During the Meeting

The IEP team members develop the IEP collaboratively, and design it specifically to meet the needs of the individual student (see box, "Questions for the IEP Meeting"). Therefore, everyone's ideas should be welcomed and addressed. To this end, participants should not feel rushed, "educationese" and abbreviations should not be used without explaining their meaning, and someone should take detailed notes about what is said and decided. Record keeping during the meeting is a very important part of the process. This will provide you with an accurate record, which will come in handy in the event there is some disagreement about what transpired during the meeting.

Make sure the parents understand the definition and purpose of the IEP: This education program exists for this student only. A student with a similar disability very well might have different goals and objectives. To ensure that the parents or guardians are truly involved as members of the IEP team:

- Encourage their input and questions.

- Note that the evaluation of this plan will take place over the course of the year, and if they find that things are not working as planned, you can schedule another IEP meeting.

- Introduce everyone in the room, describing the different roles these individuals will play in the student's education.

- If you are presenting a draft of the IEP to the parents, stress that the draft is only a recommendation and can be revised and improved as needed; encourage their suggestions.

Questions for the IEP Meeting

- What is the student's present level of performance?

- What are the academic areas in which this student needs assistance?

- What are the social or emotional areas with which this student needs assistance?

- How much time will this student spend in the general education classroom? For students who will not be included in the general education classroom, what is the plan to enhance their interaction with typically developing peers?

- When will the IEP be evaluated? *(Note.* Every IEP must be evaluated at least annually. Families also need to be aware of how their students are doing in relation to IEP goals as frequently as those of students without IEPs. This means that if other students in the school get a report card every 9 weeks, then the school should also provide reports on IEP progress to families of students with disabilities every 9 weeks.)

Some families will come to the meeting and say, "Where do I sign?" They may not want to spend the time in the meeting, may simply trust the school and district to make all decisions, or—because they have been through the process so many times—may simply be tired of attending the same meetings with the same people. Whatever the reason, encourage them to stay long enough for you to be confident that they understand what is going on. Your goal for families is to ensure that, as a result of the IEP meeting, they understand why the student needs special education services, who will be providing the services and in what setting, the duration of the services and schedule for evaluation, how much time the student will spend in the general education setting, and what other services the student will receive.

On the other hand, there might be parents who know special education law better than the attorney for your district, and they have been living the law with their child for many years. Still other parents might bring an advocate along with them to help them make sense of the meeting or better understand what is being recommended and decided. For some principals or leaders of IEP meetings, advocates can seem scary. If you have talked with the individuals active in this student's life, have a clear understanding of the report issued by the multidisciplinary team, and ensure that the meeting addresses essential questions, you should be prepared. The purpose of the IEP is to work to meet the student's needs based on the report generated by the team. The principal should make every effort to keep everyone focused on that goal.

Bear in mind that it might take more than one session to complete the IEP. However, to ensure that the meeting runs as efficiently as possible: Keep the participants focused on the goals and objectives included in the IEP, review what has worked during the past year, and discuss the changes for next year's IEP. Every IEP should include all the necessary components as required by law, and:

- Link goals and objectives,
- Link specially designed instruction to the evaluation data,
- Include input from the parent or guardian,
- Be the result of a team effort (including general education teacher, special educator, and others knowledgeable about the student and/or disability).

If you hold the meeting in an office in which there might questions of privacy, consider changing the location. Make sure all participants have the opportunity to sit in comfortable chairs, that water is provided to the attendees, and that a break is provided if the meeting takes over an hour. Make sure the room is as free from distractions as possible, such as a ringing telephone, fax machine, or copy machine use. If by chance there are individuals who cannot be there, explore including them via a speaker telephone or online meeting program (e.g., WebEx, GoToMeeting, Skype) to facilitate their involvement. Because the development of the IEP is a team process, use a chalkboard, easel with paper, or interactive whiteboard to generate and organize ideas and suggestions. After the IEP has been developed and approved, and everyone on the team has signed it, provide copies to the student's parents or guardians and to any team member involved in its implementation.

After the Meeting

Getting the IEP signed by all parties who will be working with the student is an important part of the process. However, the most important part of the process is to make sure that the IEP is working to meet the student's needs. Figure 4.2 provides a checklist for following the implementation of a student's IEP; it is helpful to document all these steps with at least a brief summary of the conversations that you have had with the teachers, the dates of meetings, and the timing of reports and communications. Make sure that teachers do not view your IEP progress meetings as punitive or paternalistic, but rather as a means of checking the progress of the student. Consider whether changes need to be made (e.g., additional time and services, reduced time and services).

	Figure 4.2 Checklist for IEP Progress Monitoring
	Talk with each of the teachers in your building who are working to implement IEPs monthly about every student. Are all these students' needs being met?
	At least once every 9 weeks meet with the special education teachers and determine if students with IEPs are making progress toward their IEP goals.
	Ensure notices are sent to families about special educations students' progress on IEP goals as frequently as the school sends other grade and progress reports. IEP progress reports could say that the goal is met or being addressed, that the student is at ___% competency, or that the goal has not been attempted. Not every IEP goal is necessarily addressed during each marking period.
	If a student is not meeting the goals of the IEP, or changes appear to be required, arrange for another IEP meeting as soon as possible.

IEPs From Other Districts

If a student arrives at your school with an IEP from another district, you are obligated to implement services comparable to those described in the existing IEP until:

- Your school formally adopts (with parent or guardian agreement) the existing IEP, or

- Your school district develops and implements a new IEP (34 C.F.R. § 300.323[f]).

This can make planning difficult, if a student enters your district when the school year is well underway. However, regardless of how well your district is financed, you must meet incoming students' needs.

If a child moves into your district with an IEP, you must implement that existing IEP. The IEP the student brought is valid until a new IEP is developed. You cannot change the education and interventions provided to the student just because he or she is starting in your school. For instance, you cannot take a child receiving services for a learning disability in a self-contained day school in the previous district and switch him into a general education classroom setting with only intermittent supports. You may rewrite the IEP to reflect the specifics of your building and your personnel and you can use information in the previous IEP and any supporting reports and school records in developing the new IEP.

Working With Families

As we have mentioned, schools must make a concerted attempt to involve families of students with disabilities in the IEP development process and document these efforts (see box, "Recommended Documentation"). In addition, make every effort to ensure families understand what is going on during IEP meetings. Take time during the meeting to make sure families understand the process, the terminology, and the settings in which the student will be educated and for what purpose.

What if the Parent or Guardian Does Not Sign the IEP?

There are many reasons why families may be reluctant to sign an IEP. They might not like the idea of "labeling" their child as requiring special education services, they might not want the student educated outside of the general education classroom, or they might want more educational interventions than what your team has proposed. An important point to remember is that families may have a very good reason for this reluctance. The first thing to do is determine why they have refused to sign the IEP. The reasons for their actions will steer your next steps, and will help your district in making decisions about the best response.

Recommended Documentation

Both as a monitoring device and to develop and maintain a historical record, document contact with and information sent to families of students with special education needs, such as:

- Record of phone calls made or attempted, when they occurred and by whom, and any results of those calls.

- Copies of letters, notes, or e-mails sent to families regarding IEP meetings, with a description or copy of the response.

- Record of visits to the student's home or parent or guardian's place of work (in the event other attempts to contact them have been unsuccessful). Include descriptions of time, date, who made the visit, and the results of any conversations about the student and the educational services to be provided.

If the parents refuse to sign the IEP because they feel their child does not have a disability, first review the evaluation reports that describe the characteristics of the disability and basis for diagnosis or identification. Second, explain that the purpose of the IEP meeting is to develop an education plan based on the decisions made at the earlier multidisciplinary meeting. If the parents are unhappy with the results of the initial evaluation meeting, tell them they have the right to an independent evaluation that may assist in providing information about other school-related problems their child might be having. For more discussion on issues related to independent evaluations, see Chapter 3.

If the parents refuse to sign the IEP because they do not want their child to receive services in a setting other than the general education classroom, explain to them the reasoning behind the use of a teacher in a resource or self-contained setting. In addition, analyze the structure of how you are providing services to students with disabilities:

- Can the same services be provided to the student (and others who might be having problems) in the general education classroom, with support?

- Can you meet the needs of students with disabilities through co-teaching within the general education setting?

- Alternatively, do certain students require intensive support in a setting other than the general education classroom? Is a separate location necessary?

For more information about ways of analyzing issues relating to inclusion, see Chapter 5.

If parents do not sign the IEP because they feel you are not providing the level of special education intervention that they feel is necessary, you need to explain the rationale behind your recommendations. If you are recommending the student be supported by a special education teacher for only part of the school day, explain that the goal is for the student to receive education alongside typically developing peers to the maximum extent possible. If the student is receiving special education services in a self-contained classroom and the parents request a more restrictive setting, describe the rationale behind the class being located in the neighborhood or "base" school. Always stress that if the student encounters problems based on the education setting, the IEP can be reviewed during the school year and reworked to incorporate a different setting.

> *If the family is reluctant to sign the IEP, analyze the educational interventions and services that you are recommending for this student. Are they appropriate?*

Another approach is to identify areas of agreement. For instance, everyone on the IEP team might agree that the student needs speech therapy on a regular basis; the disagreement is whether assistance for reading is necessary. If this is the case, write an IEP for the areas of agreement, while separately listing areas of disagreement to resolve, and then implement the agreed-upon IEP.

If disagreements exist over major issues, remind the parents of their right for mediation, complaint, or a due process hearing. (The district has the same rights.) An important point to remember about implementation of the IEP is that if there is an ongoing due process hearing, the previous IEP or the IEP which the parents signed is the IEP that is in place pending the hearing officer's decision.

For instance, if the student is receiving services within the general education classroom and a disagreement exists over this placement, the child is to remain in the general education setting until the final decision, unless the parties agree otherwise. This also holds true for students receiving services in an alternative setting before the attempted development of a new IEP: they would remain in this setting until the final decision by the hearing officer—and this is true even if the decision takes months to reach.

Advice From a Parent

Know my child's name. Our children are not just "the kids with disabilities." They play sports and video games, watch TV, eat snacks, and bicker with their siblings—just like other children.

Admit when you don't know something. We expect the principal to know a lot more than others in the building, but we don't expect you to know everything.

Be a model to others. Many teachers, students, and parents will emulate your behavior. If you don't like children with disabilities it will come through in your actions and your words, and this will set a tone for the rest of the building.

Include our kids completely, during assemblies and outings and in extracurricular activities. Make them a part of the school. Make sure they are not afterthoughts.

Use the right language. It may seem picky, but the language you use is very important and conveys a lot of meaning to everyone.

Come to meetings. Your being there tells us you care.

Answer our e-mails and phone messages. If we take the time, because it is important for our child, please take the time to answer our e-mails and phone messages (even if you do not know the answer or are waiting on information from others).

Support the teachers. We realize that students with disabilities may take up more of a teacher's time and energy than other students. Please make sure the teachers have the support to provide the services and when they have needs, these are addressed.

Protect our family's privacy. You will learn a lot about our children, our family, and other families who have children with disabilities. Please only share this information on a "need to know" basis.

See the student, not the disability. Our children try their best every day (even though it might not always seem that way). Their disabilities are not their whole identity, just a part of who they are, and the part that defines the type of support they need.

Always keep foremost in mind what is in the best interest of the student; to be able to do this, you need to know the individual student's situation and goals. Being involved in this way sends the message to families that the school really only wants what is best for all students, rather than being concerned about a line item in the county's budget (see box, "Advice From a Parent").

Involving Students

Students 16 years of age and older need to be involved in the development of their IEP. Why 16? This is the age the regulations state we must start to develop a postsecondary transition plan as a part of the student's IEP (34 C.F.R. § 300.321[b] [1]). A transition plan is the enumeration of the steps and goals for the student's postsecondary life, and the specific methods to assist the student in achieving those goals. (See discussion of transition planning as an IEP component later in this chapter.)

Components of the IEP

Federal regulations are very specific about what needs to be included as a part of the student's IEP. Your state may have additional rules or regulations as a part of the process, but it at least needs to include the elements described in Table 4.2.

Note that, as needed by the child, the IEP also may include:

- Behavior programs
- English as a second language services
- Specialized services for students with visual impairments, or for those who are deaf or hard of hearing
- Assistive devices and services
- Vocational program
- Extended school year (ESY) services
- Adaptive physical education
- Transition planning
- Delineation of response to other health concerns

Table 4.2 Components of the IEP	
Current educational level	What are the student's current levels of academic achievement and functional performance? What can we learn from the latest evaluations? What can the student's teachers and family add to descriptions of performance? Can the student learn and progress in the general education curriculum?
Measurable academic and functional annual goals	What does the IEP team want the student to learn this year? What goals are needed for the child to be involved in and progress in the general education curriculum? Do the goals reflect all the student's disability-related needs?
Short-term objectives	For students who are going to take alternative assessments, does the IEP contain descriptions of the benchmarks or short-term objectives the child should meet throughout the year? (Note that this is not required for students not taking alternative assessments.)
Specific special education to be provided	What specialized instruction, methods, and strategies will be used by school personnel to help the student progress towards the identified goals, to be involved and make progress in the general education curriculum, and to participate in extracurricular and nonacademic activities? In what setting(s) will services be provided?
Type, amount, and frequency of related services	What types of related services (e.g., transportation; physical, occupational, or speech therapy) does the student require? How often and with what frequency will such services be provided?
Supplementary aids, services, and modifications	Are changes to the program or extra supports needed to help the student succeed in general education or content-area classes? What extra help will be provided to the student and to the student's teacher(s) to ensure the student makes progress toward annual goals, is involved and progresses in the general curriculum, is educated alongside typically developing peers, and participates in state- and districtwide assessments?
Dates services begin and end	When will the services begin? Will all the services continue through the school year?

Table 4.2 (continued) Components of the IEP	
How to determine if the child is making progress	Are the annual goals and short-term objectives really measurable? How will the IEP team measure student progress? How and when will the student's family be informed of progress toward IEP goals?
Programs and activities with peers	If the child will not be educated in the general education setting for the full school day, during which parts of the school day will the student be with typically developing peers?
Amount of special education	Does the student require special education services for only some part of the day? Most of the day? All of the day?
Type of services	What type of special education service does the child need? What type of support does the child need?
Location	What school and setting is recommended for the child? Can all the services on the IEP be delivered in that school? Is there any reason the IEP cannot be implemented in the student's neighborhood school? Is the placement as close to the home as possible?

Present Level of Performance

The student's present level of performance is often the first item of business addressed in an IEP meeting. If the participants can agree to the student's current level of functioning, then development of the measurable academic and functional annual goals and short-term objectives will be much easier. The present level of performance should include statements describing the academic or behavioral levels of the student so the members of the IEP understand why this student needs an IEP. These statements might include the academic areas in which this student has problems, the student's strengths, areas this student might need assistance in mobility or daily living, and a description of prevocational or vocational skills—and always how the student's progress relates to the general education curriculum. The use of test scores is appropriate, but not in isolation; if one uses test scores (e.g., a 4.5 grade-equivalent score on a standardized test), some explanation is required both regarding what the score means and to clarify the strengths and weaknesses the student exhibits. The use

*It is all right to use a label such as **learning disability** or **intellectual disability**. However, it is not all right to use labels in place of more complete descriptors.*

of curriculum-based measures is encouraged; however, you should provide descriptors of how these measures are taken, and what the scores really mean. For example, stating the student is on "Level 8" may mean nothing to others who might be working to implement the IEP. Any statements that comprise the present level of performance should be written as a means of helping the student. Students with disabilities are often highly transient. Write the present levels of performance so that other school staff can look at the IEP and be able to make two statements:

1. I really know this student's level of performance, and knowing this will make implementing this student's IEP easier in my district; and
2. The individual who led the meeting in the development of the IEP really knows his or her information.

If the forms your district is using are too limited to include the all the information described in Table 4.2, add additional sheets. You really will benefit the student by including as much as you can.

The information for the present level of performance should come directly from the report issued by the multidisciplinary team. It should also incorporate information gathered from the questions you ask before the meeting from members of the multidisciplinary team and previous classroom teachers, and from observations you (and others) have made of the student in the classroom. If you need assistance in determining present levels of performance from the report written by the multidisciplinary team, make sure you ask questions prior the IEP meeting. For instance, if you are going to be writing that a particular standardized test indicates a discrepancy in the student's reading ability, you should be prepared to discuss the particular test and what the result means.

Measurable Academic and Functional Goals

The IEP should include annual goals for each problem area identified; these are derived not only from the multidisciplinary team report, but also from interviews with previous and current teachers, observations, and the student's family's input. An annual goal defines the broad area in which the student might need assistance, such as reading, math, or writing. It does not list specifics; these are addressed under the short-term objectives or benchmarks (see following section).

Typically, annual goals are the second item of business at the IEP meeting. They identify general areas of focus on which the team needs to agree. Work to get agreement on the broad annual goals before moving on to other parts of the IEP.

Short-Term Objectives or Benchmarks

After you have agreement on the present levels of performance and on the annual goals, develop short-term objectives or benchmarks to meet those annual goals. The development of short-term objectives or benchmarks also clarifies the services the student should be receiving. For students with disabilities who take alternate assessments aligned to alternate achievement standards, the IEP should include a description of benchmarks or short-term objectives (34 C.F.R. § 300.320[2][B][ii]).

Short-term objectives or benchmarks are a way for the student's teacher(s) and family know if the student is making progress. *Short-term objectives* is the historical term for the steps under the annual goals; in the 1997 IDEA reauthorization, the component was expanded to include *benchmarks* to emphasize that these are steps to enable students to achieve their annual goals. (Note that since 2004, IDEA no longer requires IEPs to include short-term *instructional objectives* for students who take regular standardized state assessments; short-term instructional objectives are only mandatory for students who take alternative assessments.)

The short-term objectives or benchmarks come directly from the present levels of performance and the services students need to meet their IEP goals. For example, if a 12-year-old student is reading at the kindergarten level with numerous errors and little comprehension, an expected service might be a highly structured reading program five days a week. Knowing this, you might develop an annual goal for the student of improving the student's reading to the first-grade level with zero to three errors per 20 words. From here, you can then develop the short-term objectives that will occur by the end of November, the end of February, and the end of May. These short-term objectives build upon themselves, and are part of the IEP's monitoring function. The short-term objectives should also describe evaluation procedures, criteria, and schedule: If a student is expected to meet a certain goal by the end of November, then there also needs to be progress monitoring addressing the goal.

One final note about short-term objectives or benchmarks: These can be changed during the course of the year if the benchmarks are either not attained or attained too quickly. Having frequent meetings with different members of a student's IEP team enables you to consider making changes to the IEP when necessary instead of waiting until the end of the year and then having to discuss which benchmarks were inappropriate.

Specific and Related Services

Every IEP should list the specific services provided to the student. This listing should include the special education services provided to the student, the related services necessary for the student to benefit from special education, and any supports or modifications to be used in the general education classroom. Each of these categories should describe the location of the services the student is expected to receive, the number of hours a week, and when the services will end. This listing should be clear to all the attendees of the meeting and to any other individual who might read the IEP (e.g., if the student were to move to another district).

Related services are the educational services and interventions necessary for the student to benefit from education (see Chapter 1). Examples of required related services can include but are not limited to: special transportation that needs to be provided, speech therapy services, occupational therapy services, and physical therapy services. The U.S. Supreme Court reaffirmed the necessity of related services, and defined related services as those performed in the school, but not those performed by a physician *(Cedar Rapids Community School District v. Garret F.,* 1999).

Participation With Peers

The presumption of the law is that students with disabilities will be educated to the maximum extent possible alongside their typically developing peers. Thus, all students' IEPs must include a statement about how much time they will participate in activities with students who do not have disabilities (34 C.F.R. § 300.320[a][5]). This is a relatively new requirement, and was included in part to encourage participants in the IEP development process to think more about how individual students could be included in the larger school community. The general education classroom is the presumed placement for students with disabilities, unless it can be shown they would benefit from being placed in a different setting (see discussion in Chapter 5). Participation with students who do not have disabilities can include extracurricular activities, social outings, and before- or after-school activities,

District- and Statewide Assessments

All students with disabilities must participate in districtwide and state standardized assessments (34 C.F.R. § 300.160), although the law acknowledges that students may need accommodations and modifications to participate. The student's IEP should specify any accommodations or modifications that are necessary to enable participation (e.g., read-aloud for students with visual impairments, extended time for students with reading disabilities). Again, the rationale behind this is to encourage teachers to think of students with disabilities as a part of the general education classroom, and to encourage teachers to provide access to these students to the general curriculum.

Some students cannot be accurately assessed via standardized tests even with modifications. In such cases, the IEP needs to delineate why the standardized district- or statewide assessment is not appropriate, and to describe the alternative form(s) of assessment that will be used instead (e.g., normative individual assessments).

Dates for Services and Expected Duration

Within 30 calendar days of issuance of an initial evaluation report finding a student eligible for special education services, the school must hold the IEP meeting. (If it is not possible to write the IEP within that period because of parents' travel, holidays, and so on, the school needs to document reasons for the delay in the writing of the IEP, and work to get it written as soon as possible.) The school must start providing the services outlined in a student's IEP no later than 10 school days after it has been signed.

The IEP must also include the duration of the services. Many IEPs list the duration of services as extending until the last day of the school year. Be aware that a school district that writes an IEP for a calendar year may be obligated to provide extended school year (ESY) services to students who might not need such services. If you do not expect this student to receive ESY services then the duration should be to the end of the academic year. Always consider whether a student needs ESY services, and indicate on the IEP that you have considered this for this student.

> Another important point about the dates of services provided to the student is that the student cannot begin to receive special education services before the IEP is signed.

Transition Statement

According to federal law and regulations,

> Beginning not later than the first IEP to be in effect when the child turns 16, or younger if determined appropriate by the IEP Team, and updated annually, thereafter, the IEP must include—
> (1) Appropriate measurable postsecondary goals based upon age appropriate transition assessments related to training, education, employment, and, where appropriate, independent living skills; and
> (2) The transition services (including courses of study) needed to assist the child in reaching those goals. (34 C.F.R. §300.320[b])

Three main factors brought about this requirement to provide and delineate transition services: (a) the expectations and the history of individuals with disabilities' high unemployment rate, (b) the realization that students with disabilities would leave a free appropriate public education setting and enter a system where the mandates are very different, and (c) the realization that students who had received special education services were not achieving desired outcomes (Flexer, Baer, Luft, & Simmons, 2013). Transition plans may include "postsecondary education, vocational education, integrated employment (including supported employment), continuing and adult education, adult services, independent living, or community participation" (34 C.F.R. § 300.43[a][1]).

Because of the transition planning requirement,

- Parents and school personnel are thinking about what is going to happen to the student after high school before the student gets to the graduation year;

- Schools now have to think about who will be responsible for working with students after they leave school;

- Schools have to communicate and collaborate with external agencies in planning for the student;

- Schools are held accountable for getting the students ready for post-school life; and

- Planning for transition for students with disabilities is starting at a younger age (elementary)—and this is benefiting all involved.

What Does a Principal Need to Know About Placement?

Federal law and regulations require students with disabilities be educated to the maximum extent appropriate alongside students without disabilities. This does not mean all students with disabilities need to be educated in a general education classroom setting, but it is a goal clearly worth striving toward. This chapter discusses the history behind the current concept of *inclusion* and how *placement* is defined, the ramifications of the standards-based reforms of the 1990s and 2000s, the legal guidelines for placement, and inclusion models for classrooms. Appendix F's Placement Checklist supplements this chapter, is designed to complement Appendix E's IEP checklists, and provides guidance for principals on ensuring students with disabilities are included to the fullest extent possible in the life of the school.

Quick Points

- Students with disabilities need to be educated alongside their typically developing peers as much as possible.

- Placement decisions should not be made based on services available, but on what the student needs.

- General education classroom and content-area teachers will need support to include students with disabilities.

- All placement decisions for students with disabilities need to be individualized.

Few topics regarding the education of students with disabilities have generated as much controversy as that of the debate around their educational placement, recently referred to as *inclusion*. There are many different ways of addressing inclusion; it is important for principals to know the history, what the law says (and does not say) specifically about inclusion, and methods for providing services to students with disabilities.

Inclusion applies not only to students eligible for special education (e.g., students with intellectual disabilities or learning disabilities) but also those labeled as gifted and talented, those for whom English is a second or additional language, and those who are likely to fail (at risk). When thinking about inclusion, focus on how the instructional variables for students with exceptionalities differ from those of the average student, and how to accommodate these variables while still benefiting the whole class.

The educational placement of students with special needs has seen dramatic changes and continues to be evaluated and debated by researchers, administrators, educators, and parents. In the first decade of the 21st century, as documented in the 30th Report to Congress (U.S. Department of Education, 2011), approximately 96% of children with disabilities were included in public schools. Further, the same report indicated at least 52% of those students were being educated in general education settings for all or most of the school day.

What Is Inclusion?

Inclusion is a term used by educators to describe the educational placement of students with disabilities in classrooms alongside their typically developing, same-age peers. By itself, it is an imprecise term, as inclusion has been defined, approached, and practiced differently from one school district to another, from one state to another, and from one time period to the next. Currently, some schools include only students with mild disabilities in their general education classrooms, whereas others include all students, even those whose disabilities are profound. Some schools engage in co-teaching practices; others do not. Although many educators perceive inclusion as beneficial to all students (e.g., Friend & Bursuck, 2009), others fear and resist teaching students with disabilities alongside students without disabilities in general education classrooms.

Some perceive inclusion as an institutional practice, and others view it as movement toward an ideal practice.

It is not surprising that many educators, administrators, and parents have conflicting perceptions of and attitudes about what inclusive practices are and should be—and these conflicts have continued to evolve since the inception of inclusion.

The History of Inclusion

The first inclusionary practices in the United States began in the early 19th century with institutional provisions for the deaf, blind, and those with intellectual disability. Although there were remote schoolhouses all over the country where students were educated all together regardless of their abilities, the norm for students with disabilities was either to be educated in their own special classrooms or to be excluded from schools altogether.

The 1930s bore the first-ever comparative studies between the academic performance of exceptional students educated in special classes and their nonexceptional peers in "regular" classrooms. This research planted the seeds for the debate surrounding the efficacy of segregated special education classrooms (Osgood, 2005). Considerations regarding segregationist practices were further accelerated by the legal precedent of *Brown vs. Board of Education* in 1954.

In the late 1960s, amidst the rising tide of the civil rights movement and anti-segregationist sentiment, Lloyd Dunn conducted a study of 50 African American students who had been labeled "educably mentally retarded" and removed from the general education setting. Dunn concluded from his research that the placement of so many minority students into segregated special education classrooms was unfairly biased and ineffective, and wrote a renowned article (1968) in which he called attention to the negative impact of special education classes, and to the growing misidentification of poor and minority children as mentally disabled or emotionally disturbed.

Pub. L. No. 94-142: Pivotal Legislation

The unequivocal turning point in the history of inclusion came in 1975 with the adoption of the Education for All Handicapped Children Act (EHA; Pub. L. No. 94-142), the forerunner of today's Individuals With Disabilities Education Act (IDEA, 2006). EHA was a landmark federal law providing access to free and appropriate public education for all children, regardless of their abilities, and education in the least restrictive environment (LRE). Prior to this Act, students with disabilities were routinely excluded from most general education opportunities. They were frequently denied access to education solely based on their disability, and students with disabilities who were educated in general education classrooms were exceptions to the rule.

Providing access to general education classrooms for students with disabilities was one of the main forces behind the Act's implementation. As a result of this new law, there were improvements in the number of students receiving special education services being educated in the LRE. From 1976 to 1988, the percentage of students with disabilities who were placed in general education settings for at least some part of the school day grew from 58% to 67% (see U.S. Department of Education, 1980, 1988).

After passage of this law, access to education was no longer the dominant issue; the focus had shifted to two new priorities: the setting or educational placement of students with disabilities, and accountability. Over the next 3 decades, as these controversial issues were debated, different terms came to be associated with inclusion, each signifying a different historical period. These terms— *mainstreaming* and *inclusive practices*— are not synonyms, although they have been used interchangeably and many permutations are still used today. Each term signifies a philosophical stance toward the academic environment in which students with disabilities should be educated.

Mainstreaming

Mainstreaming was the term used in the 1970s and 1980s to describe any education of students with disabilities alongside their typically developing peers—the presumptive placement for students with disabilities at the time not being the general education classroom. Although students might have previously participated in general education settings, once they were deemed to have a disability, the job of special educators was to remediate students' deficits in a resource room setting until they demonstrated the capacity to be "reintegrated" into the mainstream. (It should be noted that there were educators who viewed mainstreaming as "situational socialization," and advocated for "premainstreaming programs," which focused on behavior modification for students with emotional and behavioral disorders as well as learning difficulties. See Henley, 2010.)

But even the concept of reintegration rarely meant full participation in general education classrooms for students with disabilities. Students were considered "mainstreamed" if they spent any part of the day with a general education class. Often a "mainstreamed" student with a disability would spend most of the day with a special education teacher, and would go to the general education class for lunch, recess, and, in limited cases, academic content. The placement of students was routinely tied to their specific disability, and typically the only students who participated in mainstreaming were those with mild disabilities such as specific learning disabilities or mild intellectual disability. Although widely adopted throughout the United States, the term itself never appeared in any piece of federal legislation.

> *Mainstreaming was and is still used to indicate selective placement of students with disabilities in one or more general education "mainstream" classes.*

Mainstreaming was not always a successful endeavor for students with special needs—many of whom dropped out of school. Both general and special education teachers struggled to meet all of their students' needs, as they had received little or no training in how to provide effective, differentiated instruction to students with disabilities. Many general education teachers considered students with disabilities the responsibility of the special education teacher, and that these students should only join in activities that were non-academic, such as art, physical education, music, and so on.

Inclusive Practices

As education advanced into the 1990s, regardless of where students with disabilities were served along the continuum of placements, the main responsibility for programming and teaching continued to fall on the special education teacher. Nonetheless, inclusive practices evolved and were implemented differently than before. Instead of students with disabilities being viewed as "guests" in the general education classroom, inclusion progressed so that students with disabilities were fully participating in general education classrooms, with their special needs being met there, the majority of the time.

As it was and still is practiced in some districts, *full inclusion* means all students with disabilities, regardless of the severity of the condition or challenge, be educated in the general education classroom. The idea was and is that rather than having students go to a special location to receive support, any needed support would "come to them" in the general education classroom. (For students with more severe disabilities, paraprofessional staff is often hired to provide more assistance.) Perhaps the conceptual distinction between mainstreaming, inclusion, and full inclusion is that those who support mainstreaming believe the student with a disability first belongs in special education and that mainstreaming occurs when the student is "ready." In direct contrast, proponents of full inclusion support that a student with a disability always should begin in general education, with supports. Full inclusion advocates view the rights of students with disabilities to be fully integrated into general education classes even if this placement is found to be socially, emotionally, and academically ineffective.

Inclusion—Today

So what is inclusion *now*? The presumption of inclusion is that students with disabilities and other exceptionalities will be educated in general education classrooms alongside their typically developing peers, provided with the necessary supports and services to meet their needs, to the greatest extent possible. Students with disabilities are to participate fully, both academically and socially, and general education teachers are expected to differentiate the educational methods and strategies they use so that all students will benefit from instruction. A student should be pulled out for additional services only after establishing that trying every available method in the general education classroom has not met the student's needs. This "pullout" is to be considered temporary; in other words, the goal of special education teachers and staff is to enable students to return to the general education classroom setting as soon as they are sufficiently academically prepared; the perception is that the general education classroom is the most appropriate learning environment.

There continues to be considerable debate surrounding the issue of where and how to educate students with disabilities, focusing primarily on the extent to which students with disabilities should be educated in general education versus special education classes. Proponents of full inclusion argue that pulling out students from general education classrooms is ineffective; students are

> *Students with disabilities are to be educated in the general education classroom until all available methods are tried to meet their needs in this environment.*

stigmatized, and services are fragmented. Proponents of maintaining the continuum of services have discussed the lack of preparation of general education teachers to respond to students' educational needs and the benefits of special education class resources, and point out that instruction in the general education classroom is not individualized.

Federal Law

Congress made it explicit then (and now under IDEA) that students with disabilities have the ultimate right to be educated alongside and in the same setting as their peers. IDEA does not "require" inclusion; rather, the presumption of the law is that:

- To the maximum extent appropriate, children with disabilities, including children in public or private institutions or other care facilities, are educated with children who are nondisabled; and

- Special classes, separate schooling, or other removal of children with disabilities from the regular educational environment occurs only if the nature or severity of the disability is such that education in regular classes with the use of supplementary aids and services cannot be achieved satisfactorily. (34 C.F.R. § 300.114[a])

This presumption has been part of the law regarding the education of students with disabilities since 1975, remaining unchanged to this day. What has changed is the interpretation of the legislation and the debate regarding *where* students with disabilities should be educated. The law intends the degree of inclusion for an individual student with special education needs be determined at least annually; be based upon the IEP of the child; and be as close as possible to the child's home, with students being educated in their "regular" or neighborhood school—with the parent's approval and the caveat "unless the IEP … requires some other arrangement" (34 C.F.R. § 300.116).

As discussed in Chapter 4, students' IEPs must include a statement of "present levels of academic and functional performance," explicating "how the child's disability affects the child's involvement and progress in the general education curriculum (i.e., the same curriculum as for nondisabled children)" (34 C.F.R. § 300.320[a][1][i]). In other words, students with disabilities should not merely be in the same room as their typically developing peers, but are to be following the same curriculum (accommodated accordingly). This does not mean that every child with a disability has to be included in the general classroom all the time; the presumption of the law is that a continuum of placement be available for every student. So, when developing an IEP, the team must consider a general education classroom setting as the starting point. If the team concurs the LRE for the individual student is not in a general education setting, this must be explained with adequate evidence.

> *The important point is the need for inclusion of students with disabilities in all aspects of the school, both academic and nonacademic settings, while still meeting the individual needs of all students.*

Continuum is an important term to keep in mind when discussing inclusion. It is also an important part of the Council for Exceptional Children (CEC)'s policy on inclusive schools (2010, p. H-14). The federal regulations on the continuum of alternative placements, in conjunction with statements about educating in the LRE, provide most of the fodder for the debate around inclusion. The federal regulations specifically state that "each public agency must ensure that a continuum of alternative placements is available to meet the needs of children with disabilities for special education and related services" (34 C.F.R. § 300.115[a]). Further, every school district's continuum of alternative placements must:

- Include the alternative placements listed in the definition of special education under § 300.38 (instruction in regular classes, special classes, special schools, home instruction, and instruction in hospitals and institutions); and

- Make provision for supplementary services (such as resource room or itinerant instruction) to be provided in conjunction with regular class placement. (34 C.F.R. §300.115[b])

In summary, to carry out the intent of IDEA, IEP teams should seek to educate students with disabilities in a setting that resembles the general education program as closely as possible while simultaneously meeting the unique needs of each individual with disabilities.

As we have noted, inclusion is one of the most contentious issues in special education, and principals need to understand both sides of the debate. Rather than framing the debate as reasons *for* and reasons *against* inclusion, however, Table 5.1 illustrates reasons "for" inclusion and reasons why inclusion "depends." Students should be educated in the LRE; however, this requires attention, commitment, and work to be successful.

Table 5.1 Considerations Regarding Inclusion	
Reasons for inclusion	Reasons why inclusion "depends"
The general education classroom is the location where all of the other students the child's same age are educated. Therefore, other students in the neighborhood and this student all go to the same class. This can only occur when there is support for all students.	The general education classroom is not individualized and denies the uniqueness of the needs of the student with a disability.
When appropriate support is provided, ALL students can benefit from inclusion (Mastropieri & Scruggs, 2010).	Special education classrooms are often more structured than general education classrooms, and therefore students with disabilities have a greater chance for success and improved instructional time.
There is a serious stigma associated with removal of students from the general education classroom.	Not all special education services can be provided in the general education classroom. In addition, if they are provided, they can be disruptive to the rest of the class.
When a student leaves the general education classroom to receive support, they are losing valuable instructional time.	General education teachers and staff are not trained in how to work with students with disabilities. (Principals, similarly, are in most cases not trained in best practices for educating students with disabilities.)
The instructional methodologies used by special education are not that different from those used by general education teachers.	Students with disabilities who do not receive appropriate supports will fall further behind their peers.

Determining Best Placement for Students With Disabilities

There have been many different court cases relating to inclusion and education in the LRE; what the courts in the different judicial circuits have found might seem confusing when examining these cases. For instance, in Kentucky, Ohio, Michigan, and Tennessee, the question addressed by the court has been: Can the educational services that make a segregated placement superior feasibly be provided in a nonsegregated setting (*Roncker v. Walter*, 1983)? In Texas, Louisiana, and Mississippi, the question has been: Can education in the general education classroom with supplementary aids and services be achieved satisfactorily (*Daniel R.R. v. State Board of Education*, 1989)?

One of the cases that discussed inclusion in a very clean manner was *Oberti v. Board of Education* (1993). In this case, the court noted that "a school district is prohibited from placing a child with disabilities outside of a regular classroom if educating the child in a regular classroom with supplementary aids and support services can be achieved satisfactorily"; this decision provides principals and IEP teams with guidelines when evaluating the educational placement of a student with disabilities:

- What steps has the school taken to try to include the student in a general education classroom setting?

- Has the school (or district) considered the whole range of supplementary aids and services and attempted to modify the grade-level general education program to meet the needs of the student?

- How does the educational benefit of being in a general education classroom (e.g., enhanced social and communication skills) compare to the benefits the student would receive in a segregated classroom? (Note that a determination that a student would make greater academic progress in a segregated program may not warrant excluding that child from the general education setting.)

- Are there any possible negative effects inclusion may have on the education of other children in the classroom?

- If a student needs to be educated in a setting other than the general education classroom to benefit, what efforts has the school made to include the student in school programs with typically developing peers?

If a school has not given any consideration to including a student with disabilities in a general education classroom with supplementary aids and services, or to modifying the grade-level curriculum, then it has most likely violated IDEA's mainstreaming directive: "the Act does not permit states to make mere token gestures to accommodate handicapped students;

its requirements for modifying and supplementing regular education is broad" (*Oberti,* 1993).

So, the presumption of federal law is that students with disabilities will be educated along with students without disabilities to the maximum extent appropriate. Moreover, following the *Oberti* guidelines, students with disabilities should be removed from the general education classroom only when the nature or severity of their disability prevents them from receiving an appropriate education. Remember that students' IEPs are designed to meet their unique educational needs, and delineate the aids and services necessary to support these needs. One of a principal's responsibilities, then, is to ensure that school staff members similarly have the aids, services, and supports they need to include and assist students with disabilities in all school environments.

Leading the Inclusion Effort

Table 5.2 discusses steps principals can follow to lead the inclusion effort in an individual school:

1. Educate staff.
2. Ensure the availability of supplementary aids and services.
3. Provide time for planning, meetings, inservice training, and conferences.
4. Demonstrate commitment.

These steps are in addition to, overlap, and provide the foundation for our discussion about the principal's role as instructional leader (see Chapter 6). Regardless of your thoughts or feelings about the inclusion of students with disabilities in the general education classroom setting, the presumption of the law is that students will be educated in the least restrictive environment. There certainly will be parents who will demand their children be educated in general education classrooms, and you need to be able to make every effort to do so; when done right—with leadership from the building principal—there are numerous benefits for all involved (see Turnbull, Turnbull, Erwin, Soodak, & Shogren, 2010). It is better to do it right from the beginning than to go along with decisions that are not aligned with federal law and which will cause problems—and then have to build staff support and rebuild parent trust after the fact.

Table 5.2 Steps for Implementing and Supporting Inclusion	
Educate staff	Ensure that staff members understand the **presumption of the law**, which is • That students with disabilities should be educated to the maximum extent appropriate with students without disabilities, and • That special classes, separate schooling, or other segregation of students with disabilities should only be considered if the nature or severity of the disability is such that education in general education settings (with supplementary aids and services) cannot be achieved satisfactorily. Ensure that staff members understand the **foundational concepts**: • Students with disabilities are already educated in the general education classroom most of the time. • Students with more severe disabilities and challenges have historically been included in almost all of the noncurricular activities (e.g., lunch, art, recess, traveling to and from school). • Students with disabilities often do much better in structured activities; they have already found success in unstructured (noncurricular) activities, so can also be successful in the traditional academic environment. • The vast majority of students with disabilities have mild disabilities, but require accommodations and modifications to help ameliorate their difficulties and often require direct instruction in learning strategies. • Inclusion decisions are not one-size-fits-all but on an individual basis; the education setting is chosen based on student needs. • Some students' needs cannot be met in the general education setting. However, for all students, there must be a concerted effort to include them in the general education classroom setting with appropriate support.

Table 5.2 *(continued)*	
Steps for Implementing and Supporting Inclusion	
Ensure the availability of supplementary aids and services	To effectively support teachers in an inclusive environment, ensure that students with disabilities are "spread out" among different classrooms; consider *natural proportions* (i.e., proportion of students with disabilities in a classroom reflects proportion in the total population).
Provide time for planning, meetings, inservice training, and conferences	Students with disabilities' needs change over the course of the school year, so ensure that the individuals who are working to meet those needs have opportunities to continue to plan. • Build into the schedule regular meeting times for teachers to work, plan, and reflect on different students' needs in different settings. The ideal would be some time each day, but the more practical is reserved time about once a week. • Arrange special meetings when something is not working for a student or for your staff (e.g., unresolved discipline issues, students who need more support in unstructured activities or environments). • Schedule meeting times to best fit with teachers' other planning and instructional times. • Involve educational staff in planning how to support individual students, and how to collaborate to support students with disabilities in the school. • Identify teachers' professional development needs and create inserve training to meet those needs, or identify conferences and workshops they can attend.
Demonstrate commitment	Ways of demonstrating the commitment include • attending and participating in IEP meetings, • asking questions about how students are doing, • reinforcing positives when students with disabilities are working effectively, and • reinforcing positives when special education teachers and other staff are working together to meet the needs of students with disabilities.

When **educating staff**, it is important that general education classroom and content-area teachers understand that inclusion does not mean that students with disabilities will be "dumped" into their classrooms without support, that support will be provided. General education teachers may need to make changes in the methods and materials they use, however, to ensure that students with disabilities receive an appropriate education (see Friend & Bursuck, 2009).

To **support staff** in an inclusive environment, ensure *natural proportions* when reviewing class compositions. For example, the prevalence rate for students with learning disabilities is that of 5% to 6% of the total population (U.S. Department of Education, 2011). Therefore, you would work to keep that same proportion of students with learning disabilities in a general education classroom, or in a class of 20, about one or two students.

For inclusion to work to benefit the education of all takes **time**—time for planning, meetings, inservices, and for conferences—and throughout the year, not just via a single inservice training at the beginning of the school year. Individual meetings do not have to be long; 20 to 30 dedicated minutes often can help solve and prevent problems from getting out of hand. You should plan time for teachers' professional development, and professional development opportunities should be tied to the needs of your staff. At conferences, staff can hear more about the latest trends in the field, and they can visit with other teachers who are trying to solve similar problems and hear what happens in other districts. These types of opportunities should not be limited to just special educators; all staff members need information about the latest changes, strategies, and tools, and opportunities to share ideas with others in the field

The most important thing about working with students with disabilities in your school is a concerted **commitment** to work to provide for their education. As discussed in the Introduction, as principal you are responsible for the education of all students in the school. Ensuring the inclusion of students with disabilities in appropriate academic environments and in school activities is part of that responsibility.

What Is the Principal's Role as Instructional Leader?

This chapter discusses how principals can be instructional leaders for all teachers and students. It discusses the basics of instructional leadership; attributes of instructional leadership; and the relationship between teaching, learning, and the curriculum. It also includes steps on how to improve school climate, a discussion of co-teaching, and considerations regarding the use of special education teachers that all principals needs to address. Appendix A includes additional online resources for the topics discussed in this chapter.

Quick Points

- The main points of instructional leadership for general education teachers also apply to special education teachers.

- Successful instructional leadership requires both an important knowledge base and interpersonal skills.

- Instructional leadership can help support continuous school improvement.

- The Common Core State Standards are changing how teachers deliver instruction. Principals need to be aware of the changes in expectations for all students and teachers.

- Principals need to establish and nurture a climate of acceptance, belonging, and achievement for all students.

The role of the principal has changed significantly since the 1970s. Not only does the community expect the school principal to be responsible for instructional leadership, but principals must also manage a whole new set of conditions and requirements that have been handed over to schools in recent years. For example, in the past couple of decades public schools have seen an influx of students who are poor, non-English-speaking, and from increasingly dysfunctional home and community environments, particularly in urban areas. The challenge of incorporating students with disabilities into the mainstream of the school has proven to be difficult for many school leaders as well. All of these changes have had, in many instances, traumatic effects on schools, both from a management standpoint and on the overall learning environment.

In addition, school principals have been the focus of federal and state efforts to raise student test scores, to connect teacher performance with student performance, and to reduce dropout rates. Indeed, individual schools have become the object of comparisons—rather than school districts or even individual teachers. Some states have even begun to erect signs in the schoolyard that label schools with a letter grade based on some of those indicators.

These pressures make the role of the principal more challenging than ever. Overriding all of these things, however, is the common hope of every school principal to operate not just as a manager but really and truly as an instructional leader. Effective school principals are able to do it well.

Outstanding school leaders are also aware of the opportunity they have to influence and shape the lives of teachers and students. To be a positive influence, principals must possess both a deep knowledge of teaching and learning and the ability to inspire others to reach their full potential. It is the combination of this strong knowledge base and interpersonal skills (see Table 6.1) that supports dynamic instructional leadership. From this foundation, an effective school leader shapes the school culture so the focus is on success for all teachers and all students. Every day principals have the unique opportunity and responsibility to touch the lives of teachers, students, and families. A culture of acceptance, community, and high expectations provides every individual with a sense that they belong and will thrive in this school; this culture is built upon the intangibles we all treasure.

Special education teachers are often caught between general education and special education administrators, especially when determining who provides ongoing support and supervision. Instructional leadership for special education teachers varies greatly from district to district. Conversations also reveal that when principals do not visit special education classrooms, it is often because they began their careers as general education teachers and do not feel they have the expertise to provide guidance to teachers who work with children who have special needs.

Table 6.1
Attributes of Instructional Leadership

Knowledge base	Interpersonal skills
Knowledge of child development (i.e., cognitive, emotional, social, and physical) and how it impacts student learning	Able to communicate effectively with the many stakeholders who are a part of a school community (e.g., teachers, students, non-teaching staff, parents, community members, other administrators)
Understanding of the instructional core—the dynamic relationship among teacher, students, and content	Active listening skills
Understanding of the connection among curriculum, instruction, and assessment	Able to build collegial relationships with teachers and staff, based on trust and empowerment
Access to a tool kit of effective instructional practices, based on scientific research	Provides ongoing feedback (*reflective questioning*), suggestions, and advice to encourage, motivate, and empower teachers and students
Evidence-based decision making; knowledge of and ability to implement strategic interventions (e.g., tiered models such as response to intervention, RTI)	Maintains a positive attitude and perseverance

To guide and support teaching and learning for all teachers and students, principals (and district leaders) should reflect on the following questions:

- What is instructional leadership?
- What is the relationship among teaching, learning, and the curriculum?
- How does a principal establish and nurture a school culture of acceptance,   inclusion, and achievement for all?
- How does a co-teaching model enhance collaboration between general education and special education teachers to benefit all students?

Defining Instructional Leadership

To achieve success for all teachers and children, a school principal must be both an efficient manager of the school organization and an instructional leader for teaching and learning. Management is important; a well-managed school enables the principal to focus on instructional leadership. If the school is not well managed, the principal spends an inordinate amount of time dealing with the minutia of administration and ongoing disruptions. To eliminate chaos and distractions, there must be management routines in place, from handling paperwork to dealing with student discipline. To achieve excellence, however, a school must have strong instructional leadership. A principal who is an effective instructional leader provides ongoing support for teaching and learning, ensuring that all teachers and students are achieving success (see box, "10 Instructional Leadership Practices").

---

10 Instructional Leadership Practices
That Support Continuous School Improvement

1. Clarify and communicate the school and district vision of excellence.

2. Establish an inclusive school culture based on high expectations for all students.

3. Model respect and acceptance of all.

4. Actively listen to all members of the school community and reflect on their concerns and suggestions.

5. Maintain visibility before, during, and after school; in the hallways, classrooms, cafeteria, and other places where students and teachers congregate.

6. Conduct daily walk-throughs to observe and supervise teaching and learning.

7. Focus on student learning; observe students, not just teachers.

8. Monitor student achievement and provide differentiated support and professional development for teachers, based on instructional needs.

9. Schedule at least 1 hour each day to read professional books, journals, or education newspapers; stay current with research that informs effective leadership and institutional practices.

10. Reflect on leadership practices and strive to improve.

There are multiple definitions for instructional leadership, and most highlight the importance of focusing on student achievement and providing guidance for teachers. For the purpose of this chapter and book, we define *instructional leadership* as

> the decisions and actions made by a principal to promote teaching and learning excellence, including clarifying the vision of the school, articulating schoolwide goals, building a school culture of acceptance and high expectations for all, supervising and supporting teachers, and acting as a change agent for continuous improvement.

Instructional leadership is not a spectator sport. Effective principals are engaged and involved in teaching and learning. Classroom visits (i.e., walk-throughs) are a priority and provide the basis for ongoing supervision. Effective principals, who prioritize instructional leadership, visit all classrooms, providing supervision for both general education and special education. It is the decisions, priorities, and day-to-day leadership practices that indicate a principal's commitment to continuous school improvement.

An effective instructional leader, one dedicated to continuous school improvement, understands the relationship among teaching, learning, and content (the curriculum). This relationship is what Richard Elmore and his colleagues refer to as the *instructional core*. If school leaders hope to improve teaching and learning, they must understand the interaction between teachers and students and how academic tasks either promote or stifle learning.

The Instructional Core

Teaching and learning excellence is based on the interaction of teachers and students in the presence of content (i.e., curriculum). This model of teaching and learning is known as the *instructional core* (City, Elmore, Fiarman, & Teitel, 2009). To change one of the three dynamic elements (i.e., student learning, teacher instruction, or the content), the other two must also change.

For example, the successful implementation of new content or curriculum is based on the background knowledge and instructional skills of the teacher, as well as student level of readiness to learn the new content and interest in the topic. If a new instructional program or curriculum is simply thrust upon teachers, without professional development and dialogue, teachers will not have time to learn the new content nor obtain answers to their questions. As a result, students—especially those with learning differences—may not be adequately prepared for the new learning. On the other hand, if a teacher attempts to change instruction without analyzing the present curriculum and understanding how the new methodology might impact instructional content, confusion may result for both teacher and learners. As states revise their academic standards to align to the Common Core State Standards (CCSS) and schools revise curricula to align to the newly revised state standards, it is imperative that leaders pay close attention to the instructional core.

The CCSS are changing both learning expectations and instructional methodology in classrooms across the United States; there is a renewed focus on depth—rather than breadth—of content. Project-based learning is emphasized so that students are able to apply what they are learning to everyday problems. Problem solving and higher level thinking are at the heart of the new standards and related curricula. If, however, teachers are not provided with ongoing professional development to implement the new standards and refine their teaching practices, then there will be little impact on student learning. In addition, if teachers are trained on the curricular changes but students remain passive learners, the outcomes will not change.

At the center of the instructional core model is *task* (see City et al., 2009). All three elements of the instructional core influence the task, which is based on the content and assigned by teachers to students. The assigned task should bring a level of challenge to the learning. If the task is too easy, the result is boredom; if the task is too difficult, the result is frustration. The level of the learning task should be an incremental step beyond a student's knowledge, providing a challenge that is attainable. Although a task should be differentiated to meet individual students' learning needs, all variations of the task must be engaging and respectful.

> *If one part of the instructional core changes, the other two elements must also change.*

The CCSS emphasize meaningful learning that taps real-life experiences. There is an emphasis on learning tasks where students are engaged in experiments, project construction, and writing—learning by doing. The tasks that teachers assign students determine to a large extent what students will learn; passive learning, such as listening to lectures, seldom bridges the gap between content exposure and enduring understanding. When students truly understand new concepts and skills, they are able to transfer or apply the knowledge to new situations.

In the past, higher achieving students were more likely to be given tasks that tapped higher level thinking; lower achieving students were often given tasks that required only rote learning. Teachers can support higher level thinking and executive functioning by requiring all students to complete tasks that tap real life experiences and problems; often referred to as *authentic learning*. Constructing learning experiences that are meaningful, tap higher level thinking, and require problem solving is not an easy endeavor. When teachers work together to plan authentic learning tasks the work is less daunting. As the saying goes, work smarter, not harder. When considering student learning success, "the real accountability system is in the tasks that students are asked to do" (City et al., 2009, p. 31; see also Chapter 9).

When observing classrooms, principals should look at what the students are doing—not just focus attention on what the teacher is doing. What are the assigned tasks? Are they differentiated to meet the learning needs of diverse learners? Although varied, are all of the tasks relevant, challenging, and respectful? Recognizing breakdowns in the instructional core enables the instructional leader to differentiate support and target professional development for teachers, thereby

Executive function skills include planning, organizing, strategizing, paying attention to and remembering details, and managing time and space—and support the ability to connect past knowledge with new content information.

improving teaching and learning. It is helpful to use an observation template when visiting classrooms (City et al., 2009; see Figure 6.1). Whether it is electronic or a paper-and-pencil version, using a template will help you focus on the elements of the instructional core.

Figure 6.1 Observation Template for Classroom Walk-Through		
Classroom/Teacher:	**Date:**	
Students	Teacher	Content
Focus on what students are doing.	*Focus on the teacher's delivery of content and strategies.*	*Focus on the quality of the content.*
Are students engaged in learning?	Does the teacher's instruction promote higher level thinking skills?	Is the content based on a written curriculum aligned to the state standards?
What behaviors indicate student engagement?	How does the teacher facilitate learning?	Is the instructional content based on meaningful concepts and skills?
Are learning tasks appropriate for students' needs (differentiated, challenging, and respectful)?	How is instruction differentiated to meet the learning needs of diverse learners? How is learning assessed?	Is the content current and evidence-based?

School Climate

School climate differs from *school culture*. The culture of a school takes many years to evolve; it is the belief system of the people within the school, based on traditions, policies, and norms. Although a principal can shape school culture, it is not easy to change the way people think (Gruenert, 2008). School climate, however, is more flexible; it reflects the attitudes and interaction of the school community. The climate is based on perceptions—and these are easier to change than belief systems. A positive school climate is influenced by the interpersonal relationships among stakeholders; how people treat each other. Is there a sense of positive energy in the building? Are children and adults smiling? Are visitors to the school greeted cordially? Everyone seeks to be accepted and respected, to feel a sense of belonging.

A principal impacts the climate of the school by providing leadership that models respect, empathy, kindness, and high expectations for the success of all members of the school community. Those perceptions of school climate account for the "element of mystery" that shapes the people around us. A positive climate is based on belonging. If a principal visits only general education classrooms, the underlying message is that special education is an extension of the school, but not really part of the core.

Although changing the culture of a school may take years, an important "lever" of change is school climate. Through informed decision-making and intentional actions, principals can quickly impact the school climate. Beginning steps include:

- Model respect, empathy, kindness, and patience.

- Maintain visibility throughout the school.

- Provide leadership for order and discipline: implement clear procedures for school safety, articulate rules and regulations for acceptable behavior, consistently apply consequences, establish peer mediation and conflict resolution programs, and establish programs to prevent bullying.

- Develop active listening skills.

- Embrace diversity.

- Articulate the vision, mission, and goals of the school.

- Maintain a positive attitude: promote resilience and encourage perseverance.

- Share leadership: encourage teacher leadership, establish a team approach for school improvement, develop a shared purpose, and respect diverse perspectives.

- Ensure equity of resources: fund professional development to increase teacher effectiveness and provide a fair distribution of resources to all classrooms.

- Involve families and the surrounding community: encourage meaningful involvement in the school; provide two-way communication through face-to-face meetings, technology, and print; and address language barriers to ensure that all families are able to participate.

David Osher of the American Institutes for Research and Chris Boccanfuso from Child Trends highlighted the connection between school climate and academic outcomes in a 2011 webinar funded by the U.S. Department of Education. They identified four key aspects of school climate that enhance academic success for all students: safety, support, challenge, and social capabilities (see Table 6.2).

Table 6.2 Key Aspects of School Climate Which Support Enhanced School Academic Outcomes	
Students are safe • Physically safe • Emotionally and socially safe • Treated fairly and equitably • Avoid risky behaviors • School is safe and orderly	Students are supported • Meaningful connection to adults • Strong bonds to school • Positive peer relationships • Effective and available assistance
Students are challenged • High expectations • Strong personal motivation • School is connected to life goals • Rigorous academic opportunities	Students are socially capable • Emotionally intelligent and culturally competent • Responsible and persistent • Cooperative team players • Contribute to the school community

Enhancing Collaboration Between General and Special Educators

Effective instructional leaders build a cohesive school community that is based on respect and collaboration. Implementing a co-teaching model, based on developing instructional partnerships between general education and special education teachers, provides an opportunity to eliminate the isolation of teachers and children that often occurs when children with learning needs are pulled out of their classrooms for instruction. If implemented wisely, co-teaching is one way to bring general education and special education together. No longer are children "yours" and "mine," but teachers become responsible for all children and as a result their perceptions change: The students become "ours."

The co-teaching model is a specific service delivery option that is based on a general education teacher working in tandem with a special education teacher. To be successful, the teachers must collaborate—planning and teaching together. There are different models of co-teaching (see Friend, 2007):

- One teach, one observe
- Station teaching
- Parallel teaching
- Alternative teaching
- Teaming
- One teach, one assist

Although co-teaching is an inclusive model designed to keep children with identified learning differences in their general education classrooms by "pushing in" services, Friend and Cook (2013) found that this instructional model benefits all children. To be successful, however, the principal must provide effective leadership when implementing a co-teaching model.

Co-Teaching: Two Scenarios

In the fall of 2006, Mrs. Miller, a 15-year veteran principal, scheduled an after-school meeting with her general education and special education teachers. She had attended an administrators' meeting earlier in the day and wanted to prepare the teachers for the changes that were going to take place.

Mrs. Miller began the meeting by telling the teachers that there would be a major change in the district. All of the elementary principals had been told that they must follow the laws of least restrictive environment by including more children with identified learning differences in general education classrooms. (At the time, in this district, almost all students with individualized educational programs, IEPs, were taught in special education classrooms or resource rooms. No student with an IEP was included for the entire day in a general education setting.)

Mrs. Miller reflected on the "marching orders" she had been given at the administrators' meeting. By the after-school teachers' meeting, she was prepared with a new instructional format and schedule. The special education teachers would serve students in general education classrooms: Rectangular tables would be placed in the back of the classrooms to accommodate the special education students and special education teachers.

Several weeks later, Mrs. Miller visited general education classrooms during the language arts block. The general education teachers taught their students as usual. The only difference was that the special education teachers were now teaching their students in the general education classrooms instead of the special education classrooms. Both teachers were in the same classroom, but there was no integration between the general education and special education students. At times the voices of the teachers, who were talking at the same time, were distracting. Nonetheless, Mrs. Miller smiled as she completed the classroom visits and headed back to her office. Mission accomplished!

On the other side of town, Ms. Harvey, a principal with 12 years of experience, approached the directive she received at the administrators' meeting from a very different perspective. She brought the general education and special education teachers together and explained the directive to establish an inclusive learning environment for children. Because this was very different from how children with special needs had been served, she told the teachers that they all needed to do some research first. Ms. Harvey

> An outsider would most likely find it difficult to distinguish the "special education students" from others in each class.

provided several journal articles on co-teaching for the teachers to read and suggested other resources. They would all meet again in one week to discuss what they had learned and their reflections. The principal would address any questions and as a group they would determine how to make inclusive environments work for all children and teachers. At the second meeting the teachers discussed several inclusive models. They decided to use a "push-in" model where general education and special education teachers co-taught literacy and mathematics. All students would be part of whole-group instruction and small, differentiated groups would be based on skill development, not IEP status. Ms. Harvey rearranged the school schedule so all co-teachers had planning time together to prepare for the instruction. She also arranged for the co-teaching partners to attend a conference that focused on collaborative teaching.

Several weeks after the transition to inclusive practices, Ms. Harvey conducted walk-throughs targeting the language arts block to observe the new co-teaching practices that were adopted. The classrooms continued to buzz with learning; however, there were now two teachers sharing instructional tasks with a diverse group of children. Although there were still bumps in the process and adjustments were needed, Ms. Harvey knew that the first bridge had been crossed with success.

Implementing a Co-Teaching Model

Together, special education and general education teachers have the potential to complement each other, drawing on the knowledge base and skills they each bring to the science and craft of teaching. However, implementing a co-teaching model that brings teachers together as partners for classroom instruction can be complex (see box, "Instructional Leadership Practices That Support Co-Teaching"). A principal must be aware of inherent differences among these staff members that may impact success.

Instructional Leadership Practices That Support Co-Teaching

- Research co-teaching and cooperative teaching models.
- Use a team approach to plan the transition to a co-teaching model, with all teachers and staff involved.
- Consider interpersonal traits and working styles when pairing teachers for co-teaching.
- Encourage dialogue and thoughtful planning between teacher partners.
- As a team, clearly understand and articulate individual roles and responsibilities.
- Provide professional development, materials, and support.
- Keep families informed of the transition to a co-teaching model and how this change will benefit all children.
- Conduct frequent walk-throughs, observing the implementation of co-teaching.
- As a team, identify problems and make modifications as needed to ensure success.
- Monitor progress to determine how the co-teaching model impacts the social, emotional, and learning achievement of all students.

Differences in educational background. In most college and university undergraduate teaching programs, future special education teachers are taught differently from future general education teachers. Students of special education university training programs are taught to identify learning differences and to provide intensive intervention that target learning problems. They learn strategies that help them teach children with physical, emotional, and social challenges, as well as cognitive differences.

On the other hand, students of general education are usually trained to focus on content and to work with large groups of children. These future classroom teachers learn how to differentiate instruction to make the content more accessible to students who have a wide range of background knowledge and skills. Although students of general education are required to take courses that focus on teaching children with learning differences, they seldom graduate with a deep understanding of intensive intervention strategies.

Turf issues. Gone are the days (we hope) when general education teachers simply sent students with IEPs to resource rooms during the language arts or mathematics block. When children with learning differences are taught in separate classrooms by specialists, often using a different curriculum, the result is often a "mine/yours" mentality. Today, all teachers should be responsible for the success of all students. Nonetheless, if students are still separated into different classrooms for core subjects, turf issues are prevalent; dedicated teachers become invested in the children they teach.

When general education and special education teachers are paired and working together in the same classroom, instructional decisions may become contentious. An effective principal must be aware of this potential conflict and prepare teachers to work together. Work with teachers to understand and clearly articulate individual roles and responsibilities. It is crucial the special education teacher does not become a glorified instructional aide in the general education classroom. The principal must support both professionals as they learn to work together, planning instruction and sharing instructional responsibilities for all students.

Personality and philosophical differences. As individuals, teachers have distinct personality traits and philosophical beliefs. When pairing general education and special education teachers, consider the interpersonal dynamics of the partnership. Providing sufficient time for teachers to plan the co-teaching experience and work through philosophical differences, such as classroom management, will enable teachers to better understand each other and to blend their individual traits and beliefs to form a cohesive unit.

Quick Review

This chapter addressed the importance of instructional leadership and why principals must understand the connection between the elements of the instructional core and learning tasks to effectively support teaching and learning. The principal is able to influence the school climate that impacts the social aspects of learning; by modeling respect, empathy, and high expectations for all, a principal is able to build a cohesive school community where teachers work together to assure success for all students. One way principals can build partnerships between general education teachers and special education teachers is to implement a co-teaching model where teachers plan instruction and teach together, supporting inclusion for all children.

What Does a Principal Need to Know About Discipline for Students With Disabilities?

The Individuals With Disabilities Education Act (IDEA, 2006) does not restrict schools from disciplining students with disabilities. Indeed, it could be argued that principals who do not address serious disciplinary infractions are, in effect, denying a student with disabilities an appropriate education. Principals are responsible for ensuring that all staff use appropriate disciplinary strategies that work to prevent occurrences of dangerous and disruptive behavior. For students who demonstrate inappropriate, challenging, or dangerous behaviors and who also have a demonstrated need for special education services, schools need to develop individualized services plans to support their learning and demonstration of safe, appropriate behavior. This chapter provides principals with knowledge and understanding of effective discipline for students with identified disabilities. Additional resources on the topics discussed in this chapter are provided in Appendix A.

Quick Points

- Federal legislation and regulations guide procedures related to the discipline of youth with disabilities.

- Implementing positive behavior interventions and supports (PBIS) is a proactive approach to managing student discipline.

- Functional behavior assessments (FBAs) and behavior intervention plans (BIPs) support students with disabilities in managing and improving their own behavior.

- Principals and their staff should follow restraint and seclusion procedures that ensure students' dignity and safety.

The Individuals With Disabilities Education Act (IDEA, 2006) addresses discipline procedures for students with disabilities, although some school personnel harbor grave misunderstandings regarding these procedural safeguards. Some may believe that they are not allowed to interfere, correct, or otherwise discipline students with special education needs; others, that all inappropriate behavior is a manifestation of the student's disability and, as a result, a school's typical discipline policy is inappropriate. The intent of IDEA's procedural safeguards is to ensure that students with disabilities are not indiscriminately removed from their educational settings and that they are guaranteed a free and appropriate education.

Disciplinary Procedures for Students With Disabilities

Like all other students in a school, students with disabilities are required to conform to the school and district's code of conduct. If a student with a disability who has an individualized education program (IEP) commits an infraction of the code which requires disciplinary removal, the school does need to adhere to district policy. However, IDEA specifies procedures that must be followed as part of and subsequent to such a decision (34 C.F.R. § 300.530¬; see Figure 7.1).

Students with disabilities who violate a school's code of conduct may be removed to an appropriate interim setting or another setting, or be suspended. A student with a disability may be removed up to 10 consecutive school days for each disciplinary infraction, and such removals are not considered a change of placement. Schools are not required to provide special education services during these 10 days, as long as educational services would likewise not be provided to children without disabilities.

A *change of placement* occurs when a student changes settings for more than 10 consecutive school days or when the removals constitute a pattern, such as:

- Removals total more than 10 days in a school year,

- The behavior resulting in the student's removal is substantially similar to the behavior resulting in other removals, or

- Other factors are present (e.g., the length of each removal, total number of removals, length of time between removals).

On the 11th consecutive day of removal, the student must be provided special education services as delineated in the student's IEP. If a decision is made to change the student's placement, a *manifestation determination* must be conducted within 10 school days of the decision to establish whether the behavior was a manifestation of (i.e., linked to) the student's disability (34 C.F.R. § 300.523). Manifestation determination reviews are not needed when a student is removed for fewer than 10 days or if removal is not a change of placement.

If the behavioral infraction is determined to be a direct result of the student's disability or the school's failure to implement the student's IEP, the school must take immediate action to implement all provisions of the student's IEP. In addition, if the misconduct is determined to be directly related to the student's disability, the school must conduct an FBA, unless one has already been conducted. The student is returned to the campus from which he or she was removed unless the behavior was related to serious bodily injury, drugs, or weapons. In such cases, the parent and school must agree to a change of placement as an amendment to the student's BIP. We discuss FBAs and BIPs later in this chapter.

> An in-house suspension may be considered a change of placement.

If either the FBA or the BIP is missing or out of date, it must be conducted or updated to address the current behavior. In addition, the student's IEP must include positive behavioral supports (34 C.F.R. § 300.324[a][2][i]) to address the behavior. If it is determined that the behavior was neither related to the student's disability nor the result of the school's failure to implement the student's IEP, school personnel may apply relevant disciplinary procedures as would be applied to a student without disabilities.

Decision Making

Principals may make decisions regarding whether a change in placement that would normally be permitted according to the school's disciplinary procedures should occur and is appropriate for students with disabilities, on a case-by-case basis (34 C.F.R. § 300.530[a]). Such decisions may involve members of the student's IEP team, but their involvement is not required. Case-by-case determinations may examine factors such as support provided to the student prior to the infraction, the student's expression of remorse and ability to understand consequences, and the student's disciplinary history.

Upon determining that a removal constitutes a change of placement, the student's parent or guardian must be notified and provided a copy of the procedural safeguards. Principals may remove a student with disabilities from the base school for incidents of:

- Possessing a weapon at school, on school premises, or at a school function;

- Knowingly possessing, using, selling, or soliciting a controlled substance at school, on school premises, or at a school function; or

- Inflicting serious bodily harm while at school, on school premises, or at a school function. (34 C.F.R. §300.530[g])

By law, the student is only allowed to be in an alternative placement for up to 45 days.

Figure 7.1
IDEA Disciplinary Procedures for Students With Disabilities

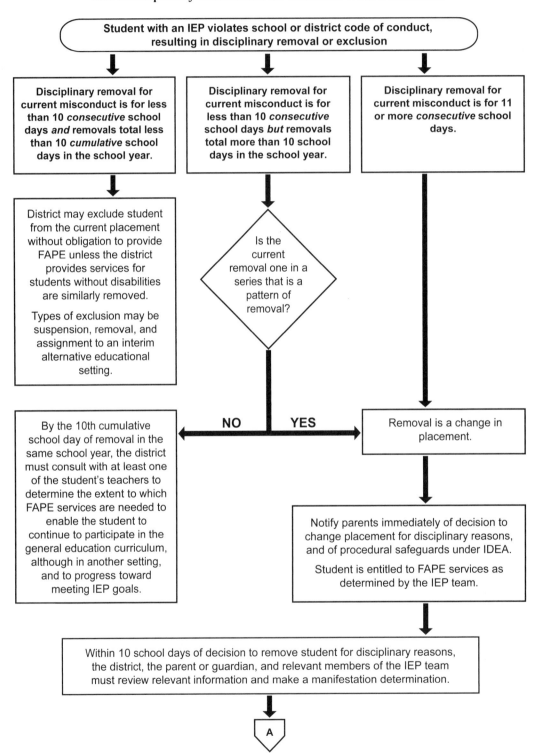

Student with an IEP violates school or district code of conduct, resulting in disciplinary removal or exclusion

Disciplinary removal for current misconduct is for less than 10 *consecutive* school days *and* removals total less than 10 *cumulative* school days in the school year.

Disciplinary removal for current misconduct is for less than 10 *consecutive* school days *but* removals total more than 10 school days in the school year.

Disciplinary removal for current misconduct is for 11 or more *consecutive* school days.

District may exclude student from the current placement without obligation to provide FAPE unless the district provides services for students without disabilities are similarly removed.

Types of exclusion may be suspension, removal, and assignment to an interim alternative educational setting.

Is the current removal one in a series that is a pattern of removal?

By the 10th cumulative school day of removal in the same school year, the district must consult with at least one of the student's teachers to determine the extent to which FAPE services are needed to enable the student to continue to participate in the general education curriculum, although in another setting, and to progress toward meeting IEP goals.

NO **YES**

Removal is a change in placement.

Notify parents immediately of decision to change placement for disciplinary reasons, and of procedural safeguards under IDEA.

Student is entitled to FAPE services as determined by the IEP team.

Within 10 school days of decision to remove student for disciplinary reasons, the district, the parent or guardian, and relevant members of the IEP team must review relevant information and make a manifestation determination.

A

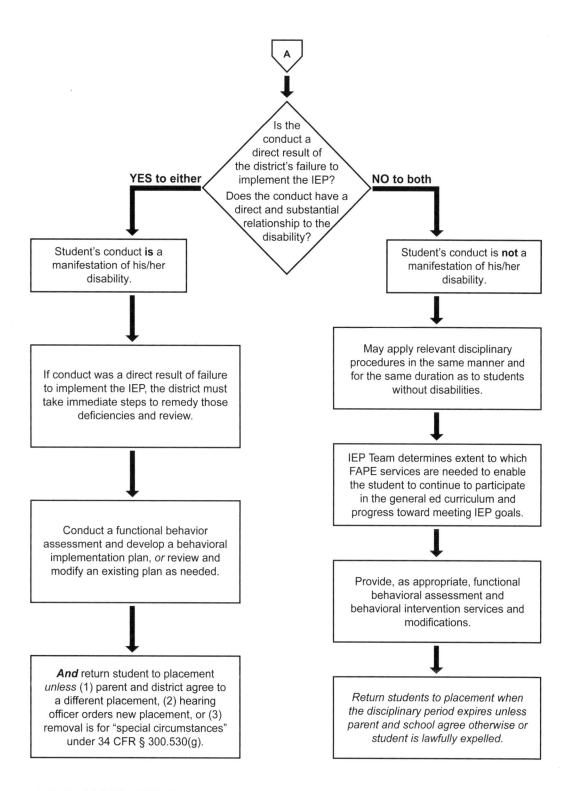

A

Is the conduct a direct result of the district's failure to implement the IEP? Does the conduct have a direct and substantial relationship to the disability?

YES to either

Student's conduct **is** a manifestation of his/her disability.

If conduct was a direct result of failure to implement the IEP, the district must take immediate steps to remedy those deficiencies and review.

Conduct a functional behavior assessment and develop a behavioral implementation plan, *or* review and modify an existing plan as needed.

And return student to placement *unless* (1) parent and district agree to a different placement, (2) hearing officer orders new placement, or (3) removal is for "special circumstances" under 34 CFR § 300.530(g).

NO to both

Student's conduct is **not** a manifestation of his/her disability.

May apply relevant disciplinary procedures in the same manner and for the same duration as to students without disabilities.

IEP Team determines extent to which FAPE services are needed to enable the student to continue to participate in the general ed curriculum and progress toward meeting IEP goals.

Provide, as appropriate, functional behavioral assessment and behavioral intervention services and modifications.

Return students to placement when the disciplinary period expires unless parent and school agree otherwise or student is lawfully expelled.

Authority: 34 C.F.R. § 300.530

Appealing a Disciplinary Decision

The principal and the parents of a student with a disability may request a due process hearing to appeal decisions made regarding discipline (34 C.F.R. § 300.532). Legislation strongly supports avoiding due process hearings by resolving conflicts through less adversarial and more cost-effective means, such as mediation. Parents have the right to appeal decisions made regarding the placement of the student and the manifestation determination. The principal may appeal a decision to maintain the current placement of the student, if school personnel believe that maintaining the student's current placement places others at the school in imminent danger. When a due process hearing is requested, the school must notify the parent or guardian of free or low-cost legal or related services, and ensure confidentiality of the due process hearing request. Due process hearings can be expedited, where the hearing occurs within 15 days of the filing of the complaint and the officer must make a decision within 10 days of the hearing.

The Due Process Hearing

When a dispute is not able to be resolved through mediation, the hearing officer will decide the outcome of the due process hearing (see Figure 7.2). If it is determined the behavior was a manifestation of the student's disability, the hearing officer may return the student to the original placement. If the principal believes returning the student to his or her home campus will pose a substantial threat of harm to others, the principal may appeal the hearing officer's decision through another due process hearing. If the hearing officer determines that leaving the student in the current setting poses a substantial threat to the safety of others, the student may be placed in an alternative educational setting decided upon by the student's IEP team for up to 45 days during the appeal process until the hearing officer decides the outcome of the appeal.

Managing Challenging Behavior

In the not so distant past, zero-tolerance policies were often the "go-to" method for principals needing to address serious disciplinary infractions. However, there is little evidence that zero-tolerance policies result in the intended effect of reducing disruptive behaviors in schools (Reynolds et al., 2008). In fact, research suggests that zero-tolerance policies may have multiple unintended negative implications. For example, disproportionate numbers of minority students and students from low socioeconomic households may be suspended or expelled as a result of zero-tolerance policies (Skiba, 2000). In addition, students who are suspended or expelled are more likely to drop out of high school and are more likely to experience involvement with the criminal justice system (Hanson, 2005). Fortunately, more effective processes for creating safe schools and promoting positive outcomes for all students exist and are part of the effective school principal's leadership tool kit.

Positive Behavior Interventions and Supports

Although the word *discipline* has been traditionally associated with verbiage such as "punishment," "reprimands," and "punitive consequences," research has shown decreased behavioral infractions by students (with and without disabilities) when a school explicitly teaches behavioral expectations (Sugai & Simonsen, 2012). A middle school principal we know began implementing positive behavior interventions and supports (PBIS) in his school in 2011; since then, as he says, "the data speaks for itself": The number of office discipline referrals at his school decreased from 1,504 in the 2011–2012 school year to 1,301 in the 2012–2013 school year.

PBIS was introduced to the world of education during the 1997 IDEA reauthorization; the 2004 reauthorization strengthened the role of PBIS in addressing students' problematic behaviors in schools. PBIS was included in federal legislation as a response to principals and other educational professionals seeking a more proactive approach to address school discipline (Scheuermann & Hall, 2012), and supports educators in taking a prevention (versus intervention) approach in working with all students. The U.S. Department of Education's Office of Special Education Programs (OSEP) and the Council for Exceptional Children (CEC) are actively engaged in supporting implementation of PBIS throughout this country, and both have helped disseminate valuable, research-based information to schools and their principals (see Appendix A for additional resources). Warger (1999), commenting on how CEC compares traditional disciplinary practices with principles of PBIS, concluded:

> Unlike traditional behavior management, which views the individual as the sole problem and seeks to "fix" him or her by quickly eliminating the challenging behavior, PBIS views settings and lack of skill as parts of the "problem" and works to change those. As such, PBIS is characterized as a long-term approach to reducing inappropriate behavior, teaching a more appropriate behavior, and providing contextual supports necessary for successful outcomes. (p.1)

Figure 7.2
The Due Process Hearing

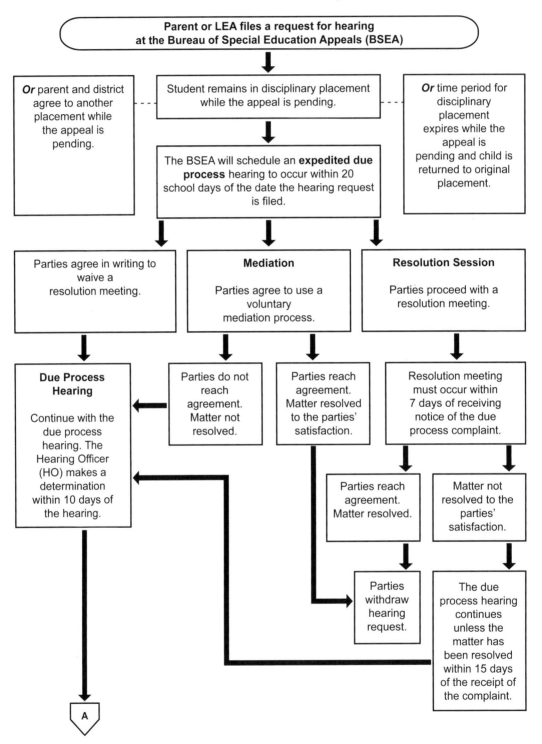

Parent or LEA files a request for hearing at the Bureau of Special Education Appeals (BSEA)

Or parent and district agree to another placement while the appeal is pending.

Student remains in disciplinary placement while the appeal is pending.

Or time period for disciplinary placement expires while the appeal is pending and child is returned to original placement.

The BSEA will schedule an **expedited due process** hearing to occur within 20 school days of the date the hearing request is filed.

Parties agree in writing to waive a resolution meeting.

Mediation

Parties agree to use a voluntary mediation process.

Resolution Session

Parties proceed with a resolution meeting.

Due Process Hearing

Continue with the due process hearing. The Hearing Officer (HO) makes a determination within 10 days of the hearing.

Parties do not reach agreement. Matter not resolved.

Parties reach agreement. Matter resolved to the parties' satisfaction.

Resolution meeting must occur within 7 days of receiving notice of the due process complaint.

Parties reach agreement. Matter resolved.

Matter not resolved to the parties' satisfaction.

Parties withdraw hearing request.

The due process hearing continues unless the matter has been resolved within 15 days of the receipt of the complaint.

A

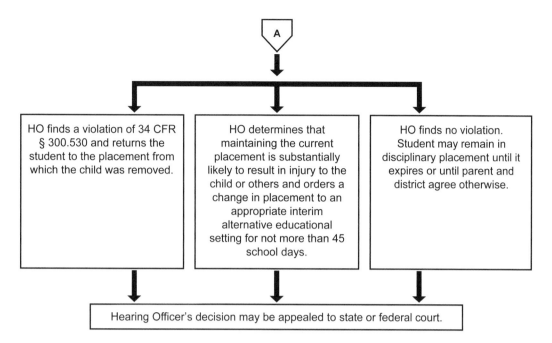

HO finds a violation of 34 CFR § 300.530 and returns the student to the placement from which the child was removed.

HO determines that maintaining the current placement is substantially likely to result in injury to the child or others and orders a change in placement to an appropriate interim alternative educational setting for not more than 45 school days.

HO finds no violation. Student may remain in disciplinary placement until it expires or until parent and district agree otherwise.

Hearing Officer's decision may be appealed to state or federal court.

Authority: 34 C.F.R. § 300.532

Sugai and Simonsen (2012) described PBIS as a proactive implementation framework to increase *all* students' academic and behavioral outcomes in educational settings. This framework emphasizes the importance of using data to make informed decisions about programming, implementing evidence-based practices, and establishing systems which increase positive behavior change among all students (Sugai & Simonsen, 2012; U.S. Department of Education, 2013). PBIS makes an impact at the individual student, classroom-wide, and schoolwide levels. To be effective, though, PBIS must be understood and implemented in all educational environments by all stakeholders—from principals, classroom teachers, paraprofessionals, and mental health clinicians; to custodians and cafeteria workers; to parents or guardians; … and to students.

Principals are often charged with solving problems of frustrated teachers, disgruntled parents, and unruly students. It is important that principals "buy in" to the principles of PBIS. PBIS can help reduce the amount of problematic behaviors in students across the school's campus—providing all stakeholders understand the premise. Principals can promote a positive learning environment by providing specific training for staff via webinars, inservice presentations, and workshops or conferences. As part of the process of creating a more positive school climate, principals can and should:

- Model valued behaviors,

- Focus on the use of logical consequences rather than punishment,

- Encourage teachers to be respectful of students' dignity and feelings,

- Train staff in behaviors that help deescalate challenging situations,

- Assist students in developing constructive behaviors,

- Use a variety of evidence-based interventions and techniques, and

- Identify antecedents and consequences that may reinforce student difficulties (see Henley, 2010).

PBIS is implemented as a continuum of support through three prevention tiers: primary, secondary, and tertiary (see Figure 7.3). At the **primary prevention tier** (*universal*), all students are supported (U.S. Department of Education, 2013) by the principal and other educational professionals. This tier relies on evidence-based practices and interventions, which may include providing schoolwide rules and policies; direct instruction of

The PBIS framework meets the needs of all students, including students with disabilities.

behavioral expectations; maintaining consistent, appropriate responses to problematic or challenging behaviors; and delivering proactive behavior management techniques. This level effectively addresses the basic behavioral and academic needs of 80% to 90% of students in a school. Within this tier, principals infrequently have discipline issues from the bulk of students represented.

The **secondary tier** targets a smaller group of students considered at risk because of their behaviors or academic performance (U.S. Department of Education, 2013). These students require more frequent progress monitoring and more intensive evidence-based practices and interventions. Principals should be aware that at this tier the students need additional time and attention focusing on their behaviors or instructional needs. For this group of students, evidence-based practices and interventions may include social skills instruction; frequent reminders, feedback, and positive reinforcement; home–school connections; behavioral monitoring; and mentors. At this secondary level, approximately 10% to 15% of students are positively affected by the intensity of services and support.

The **tertiary tier** is designed for students who need more assistance than is provided in the primary and secondary tiers. This tier requires more intensive, specialized evidence-based practices and interventions for students with challenging behaviors or academic needs (U.S. Department of Education, 2013). It is considered best practice for principals to make weekly—if not daily—

contact with teachers and students within this tier. Positive interactions between the principal and students in the tertiary tier may help prevent continuous problematic behaviors. Interventions for students in the tertiary tier include systems of care and wraparound processes, student-centered planning, FBAs and BIPs (see discussion), and data- and team-based decision making (Olsson, Bond, Burns, Vella-Brodrick, & Sawyer, 2003). The tertiary level encompasses 5% to 8% of the student population.

Figure 7.3
Positive Behavior Interventions and Supports

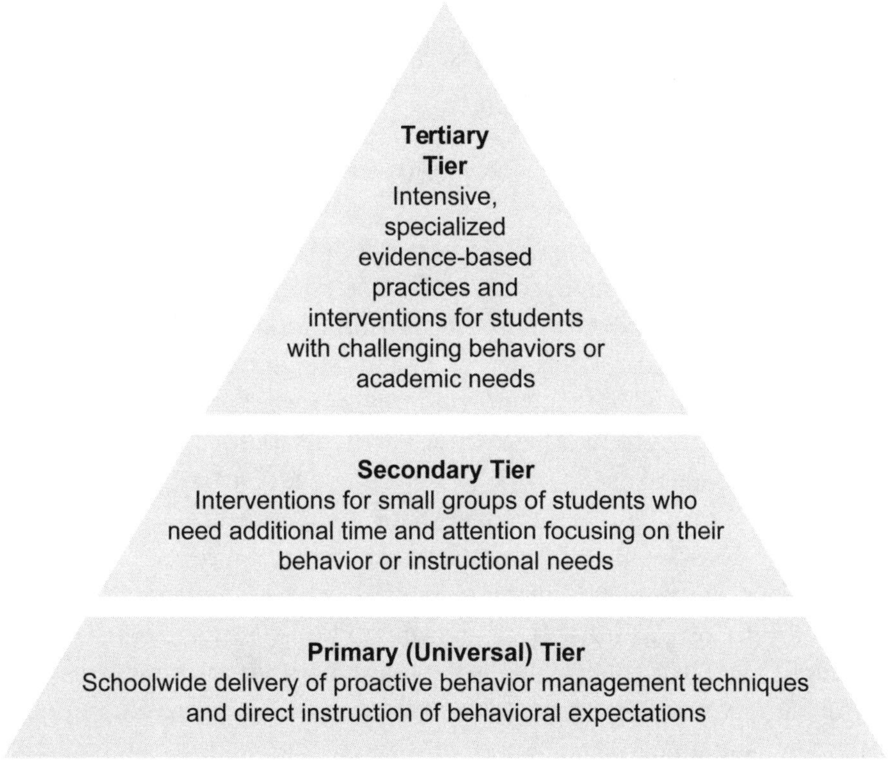

Tertiary Tier
Intensive, specialized evidence-based practices and interventions for students with challenging behaviors or academic needs

Secondary Tier
Interventions for small groups of students who need additional time and attention focusing on their behavior or instructional needs

Primary (Universal) Tier
Schoolwide delivery of proactive behavior management techniques and direct instruction of behavioral expectations

PBIS has proven effective for students with emotional and behavioral disorders, learning disabilities, development disabilities, and low-incidence disabilities (Dunlap et al., 1993; Horner & Carr, 1997; U.S. Department of Education, 2013). In addition, research has validated the success of PBIS in all schools when implemented correctly (Wheeler & Richey, 2014); however, these successes are not feasible without the support from principals and other stakeholders.

Cultivating a Positive School Culture

Culture can be thought of as the shared values, attitudes, practices, and goals of an organization. Understanding and recognizing that individuals comprising the student body, faculty, staff, related service providers, and principals often come from a variety of cultural backgrounds can assist in developing and explicitly teaching the cultural norms of the school (Fallon, O'Keeffe, & Sugai, 2012).

To operationalize norms of school culture, consider appointing a standing committee of stakeholders (i.e., principals, faculty, staff, families, community partners). This committee can identify and explicitly state the behavioral norms of the school for every environmental setting. More specifically, the committee can delineate exactly what a behavior would look like to an uninformed observer in each environment (e.g., being respectful at a school assembly is remaining seated and quiet when the speaker is talking). By operationalizing norms of the school culture, all stakeholders will be able to identify the behavior when it is happening and reward as appropriate. Moreover, stakeholders will know exactly what behaviors to teach and how to redirect a student who is not adhering to the social norm.

By neglecting to identify and implement school social norms, schools run the risk of responding to cultural dissonance by over-identifying and over-penalizing students from cultural backgrounds that are different than the majority of the stakeholders. This principle has been well documented in special education literature focusing on the disproportionate representation of students from culturally diverse backgrounds identified with disabilities (e.g., Fallon et al., 2012; Skiba, Albrecht, & Losen, 2013; Vincent, Randall, Cartledge, Tobin, & Swain-Bradway, 2011). African American males are overrepresented in the disability category of emotional/behavioral disorders and are reported as receiving harsher punishments and being placed in more restrictive settings than their Caucasian counterparts with similar infractions and eligibilities. Explicit behavioral norms that are taught to all students will likely decrease disciplinary infractions grounded in cultural dissonance. Offering staff professional development opportunities (see resources, Appendix A) can support the development and implementation of culturally responsive practices in school settings.

Functional Behavior Assessments

Students identified with disabilities may have a difficult time consistently exhibiting expected behaviors, even after teachers have explicitly taught them. When these students demonstrate behaviors that impede their learning or the learning of their peers, the IEP team must meet to discuss whether the student needs a BIP. In order to make this determination, the IEP team conducts a FBA—a process by which the *function* (i.e., purpose) of a student's behavior is identified by collecting direct and indirect assessment data, analyzing behavioral data, formulating a hypothesis, and confirming the hypothesis through testing.

Principals should be knowledgeable of the processes involved in conducting FBAs. First, the individual conducting the FBA must *operationalize* (i.e., define) the behavior (Chandler & Dahlquist, 2010; Gable, Quinn, Rutherford, Howell, & Hoffman, 1998). For example, instead of saying a student "acts out," the behavior is defined in terms of observable actions that equate to an incident of "acting out" (e.g., yells at peers, throws classroom materials, interrupts the teacher while she is speaking). Once the behavior has been operationalized, the IEP team determines if the behavior is severe enough to warrant a full FBA. One way to make this determination is to have an unbiased observer view the classroom setting and collect a series of anecdotal notes about three or four children in the classroom, with one of the children being the target student. To prevent observer bias, it is important the identification of the target child remain unknown to the observer. Once the observer has confirmed the target child does exhibit behaviors at a higher frequency or intensity than peer students, the IEP team may proceed with the collection of direct and indirect assessment data.

Collecting data. FBA data may be collected either by direct or indirect assessments. *Direct assessments* are any assessment of behavior that is observed firsthand by the person collecting data. Anecdotal records, frequency counts, and time sampling are examples of direct assessments. When conducting an FBA, anecdotal notes indicating the antecedent event, behavior of concern, and consequential response are critical to determining the function of a behavior. *Indirect assessments* are data collected secondhand. Some examples of indirect assessments include interviews and permanent products (e.g., office discipline referrals).

Hypothesis. After collecting data, members of the IEP team triangulate and analyze the data. From the analysis, team members seek to establish a pattern of behavior. Most frequently, patterns are observed in both the *antecedent* and *consequence* events. Identifying a pattern will assist in determining the function of the behavior. The premise is that all behavior serves one of two possible functions: to gain or to avoid. For example, Ms. Apple tells the class to open their books to page 35 (antecedent); Johnny throws his book on the floor (behavior); Ms. Apple sends Johnny to the principal's office (consequence). If the data indicates that most of Johnny's behaviors occur after he has been given a directive and then he is sent out of the room, we can hypothesize Johnny is exhibiting behaviors that will allow him to avoid complying with teacher directives. Johnny may exhibit the same behavior (i.e., throwing books) and Ms. Apple may provide the same consequence (i.e., sending Johnny to the principal's office), but if the antecedent was Ms. Apple ending one-on-one instruction with Johnny and beginning whole-group instruction, we may hypothesize the function of Johnny's behavior is to gain adult attention. At this point, the IEP team formulates a hypothesis statement: When X happens, Student Y in order to get Z, with X = antecedent event, Y = target behavior, and Z = function (i.e., gain or avoid). Once the hypothesis has been formulated, it must be tested.

To test the hypothesis, members conducting the FBA will want to manipulate the antecedent and consequential events. It is best practice to manipulate the events separately and collect data as to the effect the manipulation had on the target behavior. Once the hypothesis has been confirmed, the results of the FBA form the basis of the BIP (Chandler & Dahlquist, 2010; Gable et al., 1998).

Behavior Intervention Plans

The BIP should utilize function-based interventions to address problem behavior and skill or performance deficits (Dunlap et al., 2010). Students with disabilities often use problem behaviors to get their needs met. For example, whereas a student without a disability will often ask the teacher for help when having difficulty with a task, a student with a disability may crumple up the paper in an effort to gain the teacher's attention and help. In this case, it should be considered whether the student knows how to ask for help (i.e., has the skill) or if the student knows when it is appropriate to ask for help (i.e., knows when to perform the skill). Understanding the function of the behavior and what skills may be necessary to perform the expected behavior should be considered when developing the BIP (Grossman & Aspy, 2011).

Behavioral objectives. When developing behavioral objectives, the IEP team must define the desired behavior. If the desired behavior is something in the student's repertoire, but the student does not perform the desired behavior, the behavioral objective will concentrate on arranging for increasing the frequency of the desired behavior in response to the antecedent event. However, if the student does not have the skills necessary to perform the desired behavior, the behavioral objective should focus on teaching the skills necessary to perform the desired behavior (Gable et al., 1998; Grossman & Aspy, 2011).

Behavioral objectives include five elements: learner, conditions, target behavior, mastery criteria, and reliability criteria. The learner identified in the behavioral objective is an obvious element. *Conditions* refers to what level of prompting, or in what setting a desired behavior will be exhibited. Some examples of conditions are when given a verbal directive, when the teacher points to the visual cue, or when in a small group. The *target behavior* is exactly what the educator wants the student to do when the antecedent event presents itself. It is imperative the target behavior be defined in such a way a stranger could observe the behavior as it is stated in the behavioral objective. For example, instead of "act appropriately" the target behavior should be specific, such as "sits in his chair, keeping his hands to himself."

Mastery criteria refers to the level at which the student is expected to perform the skill. As much as an IEP team may want to see a student performing the desired behavior 100% of the time, it is unrealistic and legally risky to use 100% of the time as the mastery criteria. It is to the benefit of the student and the IEP team to consider a more conservative marker for mastery criteria (e.g., 80% of opportunities). A more conservative marker allows for students to have an occasional bad day without eliminating all of the progress made towards mastery. Finally, it is important for desired behaviors to be performed at mastery criteria for a consistent amount of time before deciding whether a behavioral objective has been met. IEP teams should consider delineating *reliability criteria* for full mastery (e.g., over 2 consecutive instructional weeks, over 10 consecutive data collection periods). With the reliability criteria in place, teachers and principals can understand exactly how much data must be collected to demonstrate consistent mastery of a behavioral objective.

A behavioral objective such as "When given a teacher directive, Johnny will raise his hand and ask the teacher for help when he is unsure of how to proceed with the directive in four

> *A **data collection period** is the period of time in which data is going to be collected on the target behaviors.*

out of five daily opportunities, as observed over five consecutive data collection periods" provides both the mastery criteria and the parameters of the data collection period.

Critical considerations. When developing a BIP, the IEP team should be sure to include (a) identifying how to teach the desired behavior(s), (b) delineating a system of reinforcement to provide the student with feedback on his behavioral performance, (c) setting mastery criteria in such a way that focuses on incremental changes in behavior, (d) communicating across stakeholders to ensure fidelity of implementation, and (e) planning for generalization of the desired behaviors.

Restraint and Seclusion

Principals oversee behavior management practices used by special education teachers and support staff; however, states often mandate that principals only have to be notified *after* a student has been restrained. All too often, restraints result in injuries and even deaths of students. Therefore, principals must advocate for staff to receive training that places a strong emphasis on deescalating behavior with the goal of avoiding restraint. CEC upholds that all students with disabilities have the right to access the most effective educational and behavior management strategies (CEC, 2009a). Further, the least restrictive, positive educational environments should be utilized consistently in order to respect students' dignity.

The same pertains to the use of seclusion and physical restraint (see box, "Principles Related to Physical Restraint and Seclusion Procedures"). *Seclusion* is defined as

> the involuntary confinement of a child or youth alone in a room or area from which the child or youth is physically prevented from leaving. This includes situations where a door is locked as well as where the door is blocked by other objects or held closed by staff. Any time a child or youth is involuntarily alone in a room and prevented from leaving should be considered seclusion, regardless of the intended purpose or the names applied to this procedure and the place where the child or youth is secluded. Seclusion is often associated with physical restraint in that physical restraint is regularly used to transport a child or youth to a seclusion environment. However, seclusion may occur without employing physical restraint. (CEC, 2009a, p.1)

Physical restraint is defined as

> any method of one or more persons restricting another person's freedom of movement, physical activity, or normal access to his or her body. It is a means for controlling that person's movement, reconstituting behavioral control, and establishing and maintaining safety for the out-of-control individual, other individuals, and school staff. (CEC, 2009a, p.1)

Principals are charged with providing a safe, positive learning environment for all students, so it is critical to utilize best practices for addressing challenging behaviors for students with and without identified disabilities. Implementing and teaching proactive behavioral strategies from a culturally responsive perspective will likely decrease the amount of disciplinary infractions, thereby allowing more time for instruction.

Principles Relating to Physical Restraint and Seclusion Procedures

- Provide students with necessary education and mental health supports in the least restrictive environment, positive and appropriate educational interventions, and mental health supports as needed.

- Behavioral interventions should emphasize prevention and positive behavioral supports. All staff should be trained to effectively provide positive supports to students, and be provided with conflict deescalation training.

- Conduct functional behavioral assessments and develop behavior intervention plans that include direct instruction of appropriate behavior and strategies to deescalate responses.

- Use physical restraint or seclusion only when the physical safety of the student or others is in immediate danger; use seclusion environments that are safe and humane and which permit continuous observation (both visually and aurally). Provide staff training related to restraint and seclusion.

- Develop individualized emergency or safety plans for students whose behavior could reasonably be predicted to pose a danger.

- Conduct a comprehensive debriefing after each incident of restraint and seclusion, and notify the student's family after any such incident.

- Restraints or seclusion should never be used as a punishment to force compliance.

Note. Adapted with permission from *CEC's Policy on Physical Restraint and Seclusion Procedures in School Settings.* Copyright CEC 2009.

What Does a Principal Need to Know About Accountability?

Special education teachers present a unique challenge to a principal because their work is by definition "special"—different from general education teachers. This chapter will address the differences between general and special education with regard to providing supervision, monitoring, and support. *Supervision* and *monitoring* differ from *evaluation*. When principals evaluate teachers, they are making a judgment about the efficacy and value of the teacher to the school and to the district. In a sense, all decisions we make about others are evaluative, but the primary purpose of evaluation is to establish minimal competence whereas the purpose of supervision and monitoring is to help teachers grow in their roles based on individual interactions in a collegial environment. The information in this chapter dovetails with that presented in Chapter 10; see also Appendix A for additional resources.

Quick Points

- Special education teachers' work differs from general education teachers in the areas of instruction, behavioral intervention, and student assessment.

- Because the role of a special education teacher can be very different than that of a general education teacher, assessing special educators can be very different from assessing general educators.

- Principals should respond to the particular professional development and support needs of special education teachers.

In this era of increased accountability for teachers and principals, there clearly needs to be a focus on increasing the ability of teachers to provide quality instruction and to increase the ability of students to meet basic proficiency requirements of high-stakes assessments. It is reasonable to expect that, given appropriate training and resources, teachers will make demonstrable positive learning changes for their students. Special education teachers are no different in that they need training and resources. However, the students they teach are different—so different from typical learners that they require specially designed instruction that may be delivered in the general education classroom, in a resource room or self-contained classroom, or in different settings throughout the school day. Their instruction, although based on and aligned to standards, is highly individualized, and students' goals often focus on content that is a stepping-stone to the actual grade-level standard.

For example, a Common Core State Standard (CCSS) for English Language Arts (National Governors Association Center for Best Practices and Council of Chief State School Officers, 2010) is:

> By the end of year, read and comprehend informational texts, including history/social studies, science, and technical texts, in the grades 4–5 text complexity band proficiently, with scaffolding as needed at the high end of the range (CCSS.ELA-Literacy.RI.4.10).

A teacher of students with specific learning disabilities in reading will appropriately identify this standard as the goal to which her students should strive, but she will also recognize that her students who can demonstrate oral reading fluency at only 45 correct words per minute will likely need instruction in phonemic awareness and phonics with a focus on reading fluently (i.e., automatically and effortlessly) before they will be able to meet this standard (see Frey & Fisher, 2013).

What should a principal do about this disparity between expectation and reality? First and foremost, acknowledge the discrepancy with your special education teachers and demonstrate you know they are often faced with nearly impossible tasks. They know that by definition their students lie predominantly far to the left on the normal curve, and except in rare cases will likely always be there. It's simply not statistically realistic that every child will be proficient at the same level. Blame statistics if you want to—it's just not mathematically possible. When as a principal you share this understanding, you demonstrate that you "get it"—at least in the teacher's mind. As a result, teachers will be more likely to get on board with initiatives that you are charged with implementing with the tacit recognition that although they will be held

The goal of supervision is to provide effective feedback and support to enhance instruction.

accountable for student learning, it's not all about state assessments. It's really about giving students the best chance to be successful in life.

States are increasingly using student assessment data as an important measure for teacher evaluation. For example, in Pennsylvania, 15% of a teacher's evaluation will be based on the progress students make on standardized testing (Pennsylvania Department of Education, 2013) . This concerns all teachers, but is especially troubling for special education teachers, who know that many of their students will never be proficient on state assessments. Again, acknowledging you understand the concerns and issues will help establish a collaborative relationship with your special education teachers. Principals are often powerless to change the policies or the structure of the evaluation process, but demonstrating empathy will go a long way in helping to get special education teachers on your side.

Another point to remember is that, with inclusion (see discussion in Chapter 5), educating students with disabilities is in effect a team effort. Historically, there was a belief that students with disabilities were the special education teacher's responsibility; this belief still exists in many schools. Many general education teachers resisted inclusive efforts on the basis that they were not appropriately trained and did not have time to give individualized attention to students with disabilities in their classrooms. They argued that having students with disabilities in their classes would take away instruction from the students "assigned" to them. Although this separation of services was never the intent of the Individuals With Disabilities Education Act (IDEA), it was often the general practice in schools across the nation. When IDEA was reauthorized in 2004 it was linked closely with the No Child Left Behind Act (i.e., the Elementary and Secondary Education Act); linking the two laws brought into much clearer focus the reality that all educators bear responsibility for the education and progress of students with disabilities.

The Dimensions of Special Education Instruction

Hallahan and Kauffman (2005) described how special education is different from general education by describing eight dimensions of instruction that are different in terms of quality or quantity:

1. Pace
2. Intensity
3. Relentlessness
4. Structure
5. Reinforcement
6. Pupil-teacher ratio
7. Curriculum
8. Monitoring

Pace

Pace refers to the need to adjust the rate of instruction to move slower or faster to meet the student's individual learning needs. For example, a student who is gifted may need instruction at a faster pace with regard to the rate at which the curriculum is presented. Conversely, a student with an intellectual disability may need a slower pace of instruction to ensure mastery of important content.

However, teachers cannot always determine the appropriate pace on the basis of cognitive ability. For example, a student with a mild to moderate intellectual disability may receive instruction that to the outside observer seems to be presented very quickly. This is common with direct instruction such as Corrective Reading (Engelmann et al., 1999) or with behaviorally based instruction such as discrete trial training or other instruction based on the principles of applied behavior analysis.

Intensity

Special education teachers present learning tasks that vary widely in degree of demandingness, difficulty, and complexity. *Demandingness* refers to how hard a teacher pushes a student to accomplish a task and, in fact, it may mean the teacher reduces the demand by backing off and giving both time and space. To the untrained observer, this backing off may look like the teacher is giving up or abdicating responsibility to maintain high student engagement. This is just one of the clear differences in special education. Special education teachers need to learn to "go with the flow" and respond, both to escalate learning and to deescalate potentially serious behavior issues. In short, the intensity of instruction is determined by many more factors than in the typical general education classroom. Some of these factors are academic whereas others are behavioral.

Relentlessness

Students who require special education services need teachers who stick with the content and with the students—sometimes over long periods of time with slow progress. To meet that need, teachers have to be relentless and persistent. For example, students who have not been able to master multiplication need a teacher who will try multiple strategies and develop various accommodations and modifications, supporting students until they master the concept.

This perseverance is especially challenging for teachers in the present standard-based culture of schools. Current federal education policy suggests all students should be proficient in basic reading, writing, and math skills in the very near future (34 C.F.R. § 200). This policy has "trickled down" to the extent that special education teachers may feel threatened by their inability to meet impossible goals. On one hand, special education teachers are required to teach students based on individualized education program (IEP) goals; on the other hand, they also are expected to assist students in meeting goals established by wider state or national standards.

Structure

Special education instruction tends to "look" different from general education instruction. One way to conceptualize the difference is to think of how knowledge grows in students' minds. Students who are typical learners have tools they bring to the classroom. These tools help them merge what they are learning in the classroom with knowledge they have gained in other environments. In a sense, they are experts at learning: give them a task and they are able to put the pieces together to solve problems and add to their knowledge base. Depending on the severity of their challenges, on the other hand students with disabilities often need instruction that is delivered explicitly, monitored frequently, and reinforced deliberately.

Reinforcement

Is giving students tangible reinforcers bribery? Many people say it is, but both intangible (e.g., positive praise, high fives, stars on papers) and tangible (e.g., food, tokens, preferred activities, breaks, computer games) are commonly used by special educators. It's always the hope of special education teachers that their students will learn and perform targeted skills without extrinsic reinforcement—but it's also true many students with disabilities have far fewer natural reinforcers in their environment (Scheuermann & Hall, 2012).

Special education teachers use a variety of reinforcement strategies that their general education peers may believe are unnecessary or counterproductive. Consider for a moment an 11-year-old student with a mild intellectual disability who also has been diagnosed as having attention deficit hyperactive disorder; this student has difficulty adding and subtracting two- and three-digit numbers. When the teacher presents the math task, the student resists by pushing away and crying. However, when the teacher shows the student a bag of candy, her expression changes and she is willing to try the math problem because she knows she will be rewarded. An observer might think the teacher has trained the student to resist the task and hold out for the offer of candy, but the reality is that without the promise (and delivery) of reinforcement, this particular student may not attempt the task or at least not persist with it.

There is some confusion and hesitancy about using reinforcement (and punishment), partly because the professional and scientific language used to discuss these terms is itself confusing. First, let's deal with the confusing language of positive and negative. The simplest way to think about it is to dispel common ideas of positive and negative; simply put,

Positive DOES NOT EQUAL *Good*
Negative DOES NOT EQUAL *Bad*

Positive simply means that something is added to the situation. Teachers can add desired consequences (e.g., praise, food, computer time) or undesired or aversive consequences (e.g., detention, notes home to parents, extra work) in an attempt to increase or decrease student behavior. *Negative* simply means that something is subtracted from the situation. Teachers can subtract desired consequences (e.g., sitting next to a friend, points, recess) in an attempt to increase or decrease student behavior.

Reinforcement and *punishment* are defined by either goal or outcome. In reinforcement procedures the goal is to maintain or increase a desired behavior (e.g., time on task, completion of math problems, staying in one's seat). In punishment procedures the goal is to reduce an undesired behavior (e.g., hitting, yelling, name calling). When the procedures produce their goal, we say that the *behavior* (not the student) has been reinforced or punished.

> *Behaviors—not individuals—are the target of reinforcement or punishment procedures.*

Pupil-Teacher Ratio

It is common to see much smaller class sizes in special education resource rooms or self-contained classrooms. Generally, the more severe the disability, the more support is required. In an inclusive general education setting, the only instructors in the room may be the general education teacher and the special education teacher. In a self-contained setting for students with learning disabilities, the special education teacher might be supported by an instructional aide or paraprofessional. In a classroom for students with emotional behavior disorders, there may be a teacher, several aides, and behavioral health workers. In a classroom for students with multiple disabilities, it is even possible to see more adults than students (e.g., teachers, a nurse, personal care assistants, teacher's aides or paraprofessionals).

Curriculum

The curriculum for a student who receives special education services may be different from the general education curriculum. This is especially true when supporting students with more severe cognitive disabilities, for whom the curriculum may focus more on functional or life skills instruction than academic goals. For a student who needs assistance in activities of daily living, it's far more important to learn to cross a busy street safely or use the bathroom than it is to learn multiplication and division. However, the current push towards the CCSS and standards-based learning complicates life for special education teachers who are saddled with conflicting goals. They are told to teach to the standards and at the same time to teach to the students' individual IEP goals. Although IEP goals are supposed to be standards-based, in reality there is often a wide gulf.

For example, an eighth-grade student with an IEP might be expected to meet both the CCSS goal "Determine an author's point of view or purpose in a text and analyze how the author acknowledges and responds to conflicting evidence or viewpoints" (CCSS.ELA-LITERACY.RI.8.6) and an IEP goal stating "Given 10 opportunities to interact with a peer, Devon will respond appropriately to an open-ended question 9 out of 10 times." Although both goals require understanding point of view and analysis of a situation, the IEP goal is far more functional (and meaningful) for the student. It's unlikely, though, that any of the district's eighth-grade curriculum resources will address such a basic behavior. Therefore, principals should be willing to provide special education teachers cooperation with a good deal of latitude in defining what curriculum they will teach.

Monitoring

One area where special education teachers experience a great deal of frustration is the current emphasis on high-stakes testing. By definition students with disabilities are those who differ so significantly from typical learners that they require specialized instruction to make educational progress. At the same time, federal and state legislatures continue to demand that students with disabilities participate in the same testing and that nearly all (98%–99%) of students be included in building and district reports of adequate yearly progress. This is no small issue for a principal as well. It is likely that you, too, would prefer a system that disaggregates the population of special education students in the overall calculation. At this point, however, there is no such allowance.

The frustration for your teachers is twofold. First, because the curriculum is often different for students with more severe disabilities, standardized tests in effect measure content that has not been (nor probably can or should be) taught. For example, consider the following chemistry question from a state standardized assessment:

Use the chemical equation below to answer question 2.

$CdS + I2 + 2HCl \quad CdCl2 + 2HI + S$

2. Which change would happen if additional HI is added?

    A) The amount of CdS would decrease.
    B) The amount of HCl would decrease.
    C) The amount of I2 would increase. [*]
    D) The amount of CdCl2 would increase.

This question may be completely appropriate for a student with a learning disability in a general education chemistry class, but it is wholly inappropriate for a student with a moderate intellectual disability. Current practice, though, is for the student with the moderate intellectual disability to attempt to answer the question despite the fact his teaching team has been using a different, more appropriate science curriculum based on his individual needs.

Increasingly, students' scores on standardized tests are being used to evaluate teachers. Clearly, evaluations that are based on expected student outcomes that are by definition unrealistic will cause anger and disappointment, and will likely lead to high teacher attrition.

Student Assessment and Progress Reporting

Although special education teachers use summative assessments such as spelling tests and chapter and unit assessments, assessment in special education tends to favor formative rather than summative assessment. That is, teachers are constantly evaluating student learning and making instructional decisions to change their lessons to maximize learning. This assessment is strongly data-based and focused largely on *fluency* (i.e., correct responses in a timely manner) and proficiency. In addition, there is a good bit of assessment that focuses not only on acquisition, but also on maintenance and generalization of skills in new contexts. For example, can a student use the long division he learned 2 months ago to solve a problem in a general education science class?

Assessment for students with disabilities is required to be conducted on a schedule established by the individual student's IEP. The progress toward IEP goals must be reported to parents at least as often as progress is reported for other students. So, if a district issues quarterly report cards, then progress toward IEP goals must also be provided to parents quarterly—but that doesn't mean providing grades; it means providing an understandable graphical depiction of the student's progress based on data collected by the teacher. These assessments are based on curriculum-based measurement rather than on standardized tests and make a lot more sense for students with disabilities and for the teachers who teach them, but they rarely are considered as part of teacher evaluation. In fact, the Council for Exceptional Children (CEC), the largest international professional group for special educators, is very hesitant to include students' IEP goal progress as part of teacher evaluation. CEC suggests that doing so may transform the IEP from a student-centered tool to a teacher-centered tool (CEC, 2012, p. 10).

Supervising Special Education Teachers

Special education teachers adapt instruction based on multiple factors, including the nature of a student's disability or health issues, the cognitive load of the task, and the level of support and scaffolding the student's need to acquire a skill. When supervising and observing teachers, ask questions to gain more insight into the pace of instruction for a particular group or for individual students, such as:

- What particular concerns do you have about this student/these students today?

- What environmental events are affecting your pace of instruction?

- Did you need to slow down or speed up your instruction to assist this student/these students today?

The special education teacher's job is unique with respect to individual students and instruction, but it's also unique in that it requires adherence to legal statutes. Many of the special education laws and regulations increase the special educator's workload with paperwork and deadlines that are foreign to general educators. Special education teachers often complain that they do not have time to do their jobs. Many—in spite of contractual requirements to the contrary—do not have a regular planning period or lunchtime free of students. There are specific, fairly simple things principals can do to support special education teachers and facilitate their work (see box, "Supporting Special Education Teachers").

Be aware that special education teachers often experience tension regarding to whom they are ultimately responsible: at the building level, the principal is clearly the educational leader, but special education teachers also receive support and direction from a special education supervisor or director. It is helpful for the teacher if there is a clear description of to whom the teacher should direct questions. For example, in dealing with litigious parents, should the teacher first contact the principal or the district supervisor?

As principal, you should meet early and often with the special education supervisor so you are aware of potential upcoming issues. You should also be clear about the district's expectation of general education teachers in the student eligibility determination process (see discussion in Chapter 3). The increasing use of response to intervention (RTI) to provide services to students, who in the past may have been identified as needing special education services, requires that general education teachers use instructional methodologies that previously were typically the domain of special education teachers. The special education supervisor can be an excellent resource for you in implementing RTI.

Supporting Special Education Teachers

Ensure that special education teachers have time to plan. It's not uncommon for them to be responsible for several content areas and grade levels.

Provide time for special education teachers and general education teachers to plan and collaborate. This is even more essential when implementing co-teaching as a service delivery model. Co-teaching without planning generally transforms the special education teacher into a highly paid classroom aide.

Enable the special education teacher to meet with parents during the school day. This can be accomplished by hiring a floating sub to fill in for different special education teachers through the day.

Attend IEP meetings even if you are not assigned as the local education agency representative. The teacher and parents will appreciate your presence and you'll send the signal that you're interested in what goes on in the lives of students with IEPs.

And, finally, remember that special education is a rapidly developing and changing field. Although the principles of special education instruction (Hallahan & Kauffman, 2005) have remained constant over the nearly 40 years of formalized legal requirements for special education, the methodologies and technologies to support students with disabilities change constantly. Nowhere is this truer than in the fast-moving, rapidly changing application of technology (e.g., incorporation of tablets and computers, augmentative and assistive communication). In addition, the legal requirements and practice of special education are subject to constant regulatory changes from legislatures and courts.

To remain current and able to implement best practices, special educators need inservice training and continuing education that is geared to their needs. It's not uncommon to hear disparaging comments from special educators after a required full-day inservice to introduce a new curriculum that they will never implement with their students. At the same time, they clamor for training on how to use new IEP software or an iPad app that helps students with autism spectrum disorders express their desires. Targeted training should be a focus of every building principal when participating in district planning for inservice days.

Evaluating Special Education Teachers

CEC spent over 3 years developing its recommendations for special education teacher evaluation (2012; see also Appendix A) convening an advisory group of teachers of students with disabilities in states experiencing with new evaluation systems and experts to consider the current state of special education teacher evaluation and potential challenges. In addition, the group solicited and received hundreds of comments about the issue.

> *Just as students with exceptionalities comprise a small fraction of overall student body, special educators are a relatively small group.*

Among other things, CEC recommends that special education teachers be involved in the development and implementation of the teacher evaluation process, and that evaluations be based on the following:

- An individual teacher's specific role and responsibilities, which may vary from year to year.

- Performance expectations, which in turn are based on professional standards mutually agreed upon by the teacher and the evaluator.

- The severity of the student population.

- The teacher's development of students' IEPs and their implementation, skill in providing access to general education classrooms, and measures of student growth that are a fair and accurate representation of student growth and the special education teacher's contribution to that growth.

And evaluation of their work must never be based solely on student progress and achievement.

In general, supervision and mentoring of special education teachers is no different from supervising and mentoring general education teachers; both need effective feedback and support to be able to do their jobs and have a positive effect on student learning. Special education teachers simply need the principal to understand that their job involves distinct behaviors that may be different from those seen in the rest of the building. Among those are instructional differences, behavioral interventions, and assessment procedures.

When in doubt as to the best policy or procedure, open communication among the principal, special education teacher, and the special education supervisor should be maintained. The best way to enhance student outcomes is to work as a collaborative team. Chapter 10 provides additional information and resources on supporting special education teachers.

What Does a Principal Need to Know About School Counselors?

This chapter outlines how principals can more effectively utilize school counselors in the broad application of providing special education services. School counselors' roles, tasks, and duties pursuant to special education vary considerably across schools, school levels, and school districts. The American School Counselor Association's National Model (ASCA, 2010a) denotes and clarifies the best uses of school counselors' time, including information about their roles in special education and their work with students with disabilities. This chapter reviews the ASCA model as it relates to special education, discusses the best uses of school counselors' time as it relates to special education and students with disabilities, and provides practical suggestions that principals may consider adopting in their schools.

Quick Points

- Principals need to establish a productive working alliance that allows school counselors to meet the needs of all students, including the needs of students with disabilities.

- The ASCA National Model provides a framework for incorporating school counselors into overall support for students with disabilities.

- School counselors can be vital members of the education team for a student with a disability.

- For secondary students, school counselors are essential to transition to the world of work, the military, trade or technical schools, 2-year colleges, or 4-year colleges.

School counselors might be considered "the black box" of today's schools, because their roles and responsibilities are often shrouded in mystery and intrigue. When principals are asked what school counselors do, their answers vary in expected and sometimes unexpected ways. When asked how school counselors work with students with disabilities and comply with special education mandates, there are even more differences of opinion. Principals have job descriptions for school counselors, but these descriptions are often vague and fail to capture the full breadth of how school counselors contribute to the mission of the school and support the learning and growth of all students, including those with special needs. As the call for teacher accountability grows, other educational support staff also face greater scrutiny for quantifying through empirical means and data how they contribute to their schools and justify their taxpayer-funded salaries. Moreover, with greater focus on meeting the needs of students with disabilities and the requirements of federal special education legislation, school counselors are at a crossroads.

The Changing Role of School Counselors

School counselors must navigate away from old, historic roles and replace them with new ones that address the current needs of students as well as principals, teachers, parents, and other educational stakeholders. More specifically, school counselors and principals need to collaborate to form a productive working alliance that allows school counselors to meet the needs of all students, including the needs of students with disabilities. For this to happen, principals need to recognize what school counselors are doing, what they should be doing, and how systemic changes to today's schools will promote greater levels of academic, social, and career success for all students, including those with special needs.

The role of school counselors, according to the ASCA, is to implement a comprehensive developmental school counseling program, facilitating learning and promoting academic success for all students. At first glance, this mission might seem overly broad; almost any school-related task could be rationalized to fit this description. However, it is important for principals to consider how school counselors can promote student achievement and serve the overall goals of the school district. The ASCA model, when implemented, provides a template for best practices such that school counselors are able to meaningfully contribute to the students and stakeholders in today's schools, by providing:

- Structured lessons to "provide all students with the knowledge, attitudes and skills appropriate for their developmental level,"

- Individual student counseling to help students in personal goal setting,

- Responsive services "to meet students' immediate needs and concerns," and

- Indirect student services, provided through collaboration with parents, teachers, other educators, and community organizations. (ASCA, n.d.)

Moreover, the ASCA model helps shape schools by developing and creating school leaders (i.e. principals, school counselors) who understand how to work with the special education professionals in their buildings. The ASCA model provides the ideal framework for maximizing the knowledge and skills that school counselors bring to the educational team. Gone are the days when school counselors performed "random acts of guidance." Today's school counselors are deliberate and intentional in their programming and interventions.

Principals often base their knowledge of what school counselors should be doing from their own previous job roles and work experiences. The roles of school counselors vary by school, so the allocation of duties and responsibilities is inconsistent. Table 9.1 suggests some ways that principals can best use school counselors in providing services and support to students with disabilities. What are school counselors doing in your building?

One of the biggest challenges for school counselors is the "80-20 problem," in which school counselors spend 80% of their time with only 20% of the students assigned to their caseload (i.e., the "Pareto principle"). Conversely, that leaves only 20% of school counselors' time to serve the other 80% of the students on their caseload, which means that some students are being under-served, and others arguably over-served. Granted, some students on school counselors' caseloads have greater needs than others and thus require more attention, but how much is too much? This issue is further compounded by the time- and service-intensive needs of students eligible for special education services, which do not comprise the bulk of the school counselor's caseload. Other challenges include the allocation of non-counseling, clerical, or administrative duties to school counselors, which further diminishes access to students.

In response to this situation, ASCA encourages schools to adopt comprehensive school counseling programs that focus on prevention rather than reaction, and having school counselors work on a more macro level to effect broader, systemic changes that are amenable to data collection, quantification, and analysis. For school counselors to show how they meaningfully contribute to the mission of their schools and positively impact all students, they will need to work with a larger percentage of their caseloads. Moreover, ASCA has reinvented the 80/20 phenomenon to promote the idea that 80% of school counselors' time should be spent in direct and indirect services to students, and the other 20% for program management and other school-related responsibilities and roles (Gysbers & Henderson, 2012). ASCA recommends specific student-to-school counselor ratios (depending on school level), and these can be a reference point for how your school's caseload ratios compare to what is considered best practice. For example, the recommended level for high schools is 250:1.

Table 9.1	
School Counselors' Work With Students With Disabilities	
Appropriate activities	Inappropriate activities
Individual student academic program planning	Coordinating paperwork and data entry of all new students
Interpreting cognitive, aptitude, and achievement tests	Coordinating cognitive, aptitude, and achievement testing programs
Providing counseling to students who are habitually tardy or absent	Signing excuses for students who are tardy or absent
Collaborating with teachers to present school counseling core curriculum lessons	Teaching classes when teachers are absent
Interpreting student records	Maintaining student records
Providing teachers with suggestions for effective classroom management	Supervising classrooms or common areas
Ensuring student records are maintained as per state and federal regulations	Clerical record keeping
Providing individual, small-, and large-group counseling services to students	Providing therapy or long-term counseling in schools to address psychological needs
Advocating for students at IEP meetings, on student study teams, and on school attendance review boards	Coordinating schoolwide and individual education or behavior plans, student study teams, or school attendance review boards
Analyzing disaggregated data	Serving as a data entry clerk
Providing counseling to students who have discipline problems	Performing disciplinary actions or assigning disciplinary consequences
Providing counseling to students as to appropriate school dress	Sending students home who are not appropriately dressed
Analyzing grade point averages in relation to achievement	Computing grade point averages
Helping the school principal to identify and resolve student issues, needs, and problems	Assisting with duties in the principal's office
Note. IEP = individualized education program.	

The *ASCA National Model: A Framework for School Counseling Programs* (2010a) outlines the components of comprehensive school counseling programs that address the needs of all students—including students with disabilities—in the domains of academic, career, and personal and social development. There are four areas in the ASCA model that gives structure to the program: foundation, management, delivery, and accountability. In the **foundation** area, school counselors create comprehensive school counseling programs that focus on student outcomes, teach students competencies, and are delivered with identified professional competencies. The **management** area includes the use of a variety of assessments and tools that clearly delineate and reflect the needs of the school. The **delivery** area should account for 80% or more of the activities school counselors provide to students, parents, school staff, and the community (i.e., school counseling curriculum, individual student planning, responsive services). To demonstrate the effectiveness of the school counseling program, the **accountability** area has school counselors use data to show the impact on student achievement, attendance, and behavior and analyze assessments to guide future action and improve future results for all students.

The Roles of School Counselors—Today

School counselors should not focus their time on any one particular group of students, as their role is that of academic facilitator for all students. Due to the nature of their profession, school counselors embrace multiculturalism and are trained to work effectively with students from diverse backgrounds. According to ASCA's ethical standards for school counselors (2010b), a primary responsibility of school counselors is promoting and supporting student success by working with various school staff such as special educators, school nurses, school social workers, and school psychologists to identify best practices for collaborating with parents, community leaders, and other stakeholders. School counselors cannot function in isolation and hope to meet the needs of all students. Their success is dependent upon effective collaboration with these other stakeholders in the educational process. Teaming school counselors with other student services personnel can make a dramatic difference for all students—including those with disabilities and exceptionalities.

School counselors are and should be considered a vital part of the continuum of services offered in today's schools, and as part of a team are expected to have a certain skill set and knowledge (see box, "Expectations for School Counselors"; Holcomb-McCoy, 2007; Schmidt, 2014). They can help bridge potential communication gaps between parents and schools, and foster a welcoming school environment for new enrollees. In many schools, school counselors are assigned a caseload of students who remain with them until those students transition to their next school, graduate, or otherwise leave school. Thus, school counselors are able to view the developmental progress of students over a substantial period of time and as a result become familiar with the unique needs of students and their families, and can facilitate student success with personalized assistance and interventions.

Expectations for School Counselors

In today's learning environments, school counselors are expected to …

- Possess current knowledge of educational programming for students with exceptionalities.

- Be knowledgeable regarding Section 504 and other applicable federal, state, and local laws; regulations; and procedures.

- Collaborate with special education teachers and other educational staff to select appropriate counseling strategies.

- Know about community agencies that serve students with disabilities and their families.

- Develop and create classroom guidance activities and integrate them into a comprehensive school counseling program so classroom teachers and educational support staff can use the curriculum to educate students about disabilities.

- Provide information to students, parents, and teachers about how culture may influence our understanding of certain exceptionalities (e.g., developmental disabilities, autism spectrum disorder, giftedness).

- Provide information about the problems of the over-identification and under-identification of students with diverse backgrounds as requiring special education services.

- Participate in a consultation role, as needed, in the development of students' individualized education programs.

School counselors often provide an alternate lens to problem solving. They look for different and innovative ways to help remove barriers to learning. Sometimes they can offer "big picture" insights that reinforce a more helpful and hopeful perspective on a situation. They look for positive strengths in students and help lead students and their families through the process of change. Further, school counselors are also knowledgeable about the resources available in their districts and greater communities-at-large (Geltner & Leibforth, 2008).

For example, a school counselor may refer a newly homeless family to a local food bank or shelter to help them meet their basic needs. Indeed, school counselors usually have a list of regional and community-based resources that they can share with families to help them obtain the necessary living staples to create safety and stability.

School counselors are often invited but are not required to attend eligibility or individualized education program (IEP) meetings unless school or district policy mandates their presence. It is important to note that school counselors should not be used as the local education agency representative at IEP meetings; this is clearly an administrative duty, and creates a dual role situation for them. If there are no school counseling-related issues that will be discussed at the IEP or eligibility meeting, it is advisable not to include school counselors, as this would not be an effective use of their time. Instead, school counselors can have discussions with the lead special education teacher or team before a meeting occurs to provide additional information about the student; such routine discussions will also reveal if the school counselor's presence is required and, if so, provides a framework for clear and meaningful participation. For example, there may be counseling services and programs available within the school or the greater community that may be beneficial to offer to students and their families. If there is a history of conflict between school personnel and a particular student or parent, it is advisable to have a school counselor present to help moderate the process and provide deescalation as needed.

Collaboration With Teachers and Other School Staff

School counselors can effectively collaborate with **general and special education teachers** by offering large-group and small-group classroom lessons. For example, after presenting a lesson on career choice and planning to eighth-grade students, the school counselor might work with a subset of those students who have IEPs in order to develop material or goals for inclusion in the students' transition plans (e.g., preliminary investigation of vocational schools or training, identifying specific high school course options leading to postsecondary education).

It is common for school counselors to work closely with students receiving services for emotional or behavioral disorders, their teachers, and other service providers. For example, a teacher of students with emotional or behavioral disorders and a school counselor might team-teach a series of lessons over 10 weeks during a social skills class period. Lessons would be developed to specifically meet the needs of the individual students; the ASCA model assumes that counselors are prepared to support students in areas such as conflict resolution, anger management, managing stress, communication, motivation, goals, and making positive choices. In this case, both teacher and school counselor are working to meet the necessary standards for student success.

Students who have an IEP due to a serious emotional disturbance often need a range of services to be successful in school. Many times these students and families are already linked to therapeutic resources in the community (e.g., mental health, child protection, probation). For example, some students may receive behavioral support from a community agency working. After ensuring that the appropriate consent to release information forms are signed by a parent and (in some cases) the student, principals can expect that school counselors will help support these students by facilitating communication between the school and agency, as well as assisting with clinical case management.

> *The most highly rated college readiness factors have less to do with academic knowledge and skills and more to do with personal characteristics and attitudes.*

School counselors also partner with **speech and language therapists** to help support students with disabilities. For example, a school counselor and speech and language therapist can co-lead a weekly social skills group over 12 weeks for students diagnosed with autism spectrum disorder (with parent and student consent). Their group time would focus on the common needs of these students and create a climate of support; programmatic research suggests that teaching social skills to students with autism spectrum disorder helps them participate more effectively and confidently in peer activities (see Alwell & Cobb, 2009). Through strategies such as social stories (see Gray & Garand, 1993) and role plays, students can learn self advocacy skills and self-calming strategies for dealing with a range of social and behavioral concerns. Such a group not only gives students a safe place to process the challenges they face but also helps them develop a sense of community within the school setting.

Transition Planning and Programming

School counselors employed in secondary-level schools are expected to assist all students with their postsecondary transition to the world of work, the military, trade or technical schools, or 2-year or 4-year colleges. The current focus on "college and career readiness" means preparing all students for their futures and ensuring that all students understand their postsecondary options. *College readiness* is a multifaceted construct (Conley, 2007). For students with or without disabilities, college-readiness is related to their personal characteristics, their academic skills and strategies, their support systems, and knowledge areas related to self and college. The top five positive personal characteristics linked to success in numerous aspects of life are confidence, persistence or perseverance, resilience, self-determination skills, and self-discipline or self-regulation (Milsom & Dietz, 2009). School counselors can work with students individually, in small groups, or in a classroom setting to help develop the personal characteristics linked to success. Moreover, they can work collaboratively with special education staff to strengthen these aspects that may already be part of the curriculum or students' IEP goals.

Supporting and Collaborating With School Counselors

To support school counselors, allocate enough time for planning and meetings, and tailor inservice training and other professional development to the unique needs of school counselors. Having school counselors attend inservices designed for teachers is typically not an effective use of school counselors' time, and their presence at such meetings does not demonstrably improve their knowledge or services. Because school counselors are required to perform many roles and duties within their schools, they need to have a clear idea about who their "true" supervisor is, how they will be supervised, and to whom they can go for help or advice. Principals, assistant principals, K–12 counselor supervisors, directors of special education, and school psychologists are all often involved in the delegation of additional school counselor duties and roles. In addition, school counselors are often expected to coordinate standardized testing programs (e.g., Iowa Tests of Basic Skills, SAT or ACT). If this is the case in your school, do you have a process in place to support students during this period, when counselors are otherwise engaged? Remember that the administration of standardized tests should be a schoolwide initiative, not the sole purview of the school counselor.

Improved school morale, more harmonious work environments, and positive relationships among school personnel create more opportunities for the success and ultimate achievement of the school's mission. Accordingly, productive and professional working relationships between school counselors and principals are essential for successful collaboration. Both parties need each other's help in meeting the needs of students who receive special education services (as well as those who do not). Principals need the knowledge and skills that school counselors provide, and school counselors need the support and leadership that principals provide. It's a symbiotic relationship that, when mindfully designed and established, benefits the entire school (see Table 9.2).

Table 9.2 **Steps for Effectively Using School Counselors**	
Step 1 Clarify the school counselor's role	Ensure that all educational stakeholders understand the role of the school counselor in your building. Be clear about how school counselors work with all students in the continuum of services and interventions. Teams and individuals are more productive and more likely to be successful when the expectations are clear. Use your district-approved comprehensive school counseling program or the ASCA model recommendations as a reference point.
Step 2 Create a culture of collaboration	A collaborative environment does not happen by accident; it is the careful creation of a work climate that has a solid foundation of trust and respect among colleagues. Highly productive team members understand what each person contributes to the team and embrace an open-mindedness for alternative ideas and interventions.
Step 3 Identify the school counselor's role in providing special education services	Explain to your faculty and staff how much time school counselors will be focused on appropriate special education services. Will they participate in eligibility, IEP, or Section 504 meetings? Elucidate school counselors' roles and duties in other schoolwide interventions (e.g., positive behavior interventions and individual behavior plans; see Chapter 7).
Step 4 Clarify the process for evaluating school counselors	Be clear about how school counselors in your building will be evaluated. Begin with the end in mind. It will be important for school counselors to know from the onset of their employment what they are expected to know, do, and perform in order to meet the expectations denoted on their evaluation document. Use an evaluation designed for assessing school counselors, not generic evaluations or evaluations designed for teachers. When considering the content of the evaluation, be sure there are aspects that address general education students as well as those who receive special education services.
Step 5 Provide meaningful opportunities for professional development	School counselors need ongoing professional development to stay current with the best practices in special education and other educational and counseling-related domains. Depending on their role and level of involvement, school counselors will periodically need additional training to help them maintain peak efficiency and effectiveness. This may include in-service trainings with staff, teaming with a professional learning community within the school, or attending a professional conference to further develop needed skills.

What Do Special Education Teachers Want and Need From Their Principals?

10

To ensure student success, principals need to understand the time it takes special educators to prepare and implement the attendant legal requirements as well as educational programming and services. Special education teachers have high expectations of their principals for necessary support. From the special education teacher's perspective, clear communication plays a key role in the success of students. Special education teachers are often eager to participate in trainings and professional development that enable them to explore new supports and strategies. A principal's support of special education teachers (in regards to general education teachers and parents of students with special needs) is essential to their success.

Quick Points

- Principals need to provide special educators with the support to attend appropriate professional development training.

- Principals must back special educators in their efforts to collaborate with general education teachers.

- Principals need to support special educators in their interactions with parents of students with special needs.

When you get a paper cut, it is quite painful. It can become sore, bothersome, and take a long time to heal. A paper cut can represent all of the issues children who are identified with various disabilities deal with on a daily basis. No matter how creative or great a teacher is or how well the lesson is planned, the learning process may be more difficult, if it takes place at all, unless the process of healing occurs first. Even after the "paper cut" heals and students have been comforted and put at ease, learning still may not take place at the same pace for students with disabilities as for their typically developing peers. Helping with this healing—and learning—process is the role of the special education teacher.

But this role is subsumed within a variety of specific activities. Special education teachers must have a firm grasp of special education law and know how to write a legally appropriate individual education program (IEP). There are constant changes occurring with this responsibility, and the attendant paperwork demands are great: Whereas general education teachers spend about 2 hours a week completing forms and administrative paperwork, special educators spend about 5 hours a week (U.S. Department of Education, Office of Special Education Programs, 2013). Special education teachers have the same job duties as other educators—teaching, curriculum and lesson planning, and monitoring student progress—and, like their co-workers, need to respond to the requirements of new initiatives such as the Common Core State Standards. However, they also attend and facilitate meetings and generally have more contact with the families of their students than their general education counterparts. They frequently serve in a consultation role with the general education teachers in their building, assisting in developing specially designed instruction, collaborating, and troubleshooting. And, as noted in Chapter 8, special education teachers are required by law to have content knowledge for the areas in which they provide academic support or instruction.

Because it can be challenging to find the time to write IEPs in the course of a normal school day, many special education teachers spend a great deal of time outside of the school preparing appropriate IEPs.

In the face of this multifaceted role, special education teachers often feel they do not have enough time to develop legally appropriate IEPs that meet the specific needs of each student. The time it takes to write an IEP is different for each special education teacher and depends on the individual student's needs and the amount of measurable and observable data that needs to be included in the IEP—but it generally takes more time than these educators are provided.

Collaboration between special education teachers and general education teachers is essential to truly respond to students' needs. These two groups need to have time to discuss these various needs and develop plans to respond to them. General education teachers need to have a clear idea of what they need to do and how to implement specially designed instruction for each student. All of these issues need to be considered when making caseload decisions and matching staff to student's individual needs.

The Special Education Teacher Perspective

We conducted an informal survey of 20 special education teachers to find out what they need the most from their principals. The top five needs were:

Time for progress monitoring	100%
Time for students	100%
Mentoring	80%
Communication with all stakeholders	65%
Training	60%

Special education teachers often feel they are placed into a position ill prepared (Keigher & Cross, 2010). The principal needs to be prepared to help guide them by assigning a **mentor** who is experienced and knowledgeable in special education; research "clearly shows that well-designed induction programs that include a strong mentoring component promote the retention of the majority of promising new educators" (Ganser, 2002, p. 26). Frequently, mentors may act as a supervisor whereas the principal performs the role of an evaluator. Special education teachers need a principal who provides ongoing and consistent feedback; however, when it is not given, special education teachers need to be able to rely on the guidance and support of their mentor.

Principals need to incorporate **time** in the master schedule for special education teachers for instruction, progress monitoring, and IEP development. Special education teachers often do not get enough time simply to get to know, develop rapport with, and support the students on their caseload, so this should be taken into consideration as well.

Some districts assign special education teachers to be case managers, overseeing the development of students' IEPs; however, they might not actually have any interaction with a particular student. When it is time to develop the IEP, the case manager can be left scrambling to gather enough data and information to write a thorough IEP based on the student's needs. This situation needs to be addressed, either by providing case managers with extra time to confer with a student's teachers and support team or by restricting the students on a teacher's "case management" load to those he or she actually teaches.

It is important to remember that we are all human and not mind readers. Principals cannot read their teachers' minds, just like teachers cannot read their principal's mind—which is why clear **communication** is critical. According to Reinhartz and Beach (2004), one of the keys of school success is what Hoyle,

English, and Steffy (1998) described as a collaborative culture and a positive climate. Reinhartz and Beach found that principals who were transformational shared similar traits: "drive, honesty and integrity, leadership motivation, self-confidence, cognitive ability, creativity, and flexibility" (House, Shane, & Herold, 1996, p. 209). These traits are very important for effective communication with teachers.

The good news is that, in our survey of special education teachers, we found that they felt their principals already provided them with essential support, particularly in the following areas:

- Checking lesson plans
- Differentiating supervision and evaluation plan
- Representing the local education agency (LEA) at IEP meetings
- Providing training
- Facilitating faculty meetings
- Participating in department meetings
- Participating in building-level meetings

Another recent informal survey of principals we conducted confirmed these efforts. Of the principals we surveyed, most were involved in the activities cited by the teachers as supporting their efforts. Because most principals have teaching experience themselves, they can suggest strategies for teachers to use. Many teachers appreciate additions to their "basket of tricks" that they can turn to when they feel like they have run out of ideas.

> *Principals who simply conduct walk-throughs or observations without providing non-evaluative feedback are not perceived by teachers as being supportive.*

Effective Communication

One of the best ways to engage in clear and direct communication is through the use of building-level meetings. Principals need to ensure the active involvement of special education teachers to establish their role as essential to the school's mission. In addition, principals can use these meetings to acquire knowledge about the various needs of students who receive special education services. Principals should continue to attend these meetings to keep up to date on the progress of students receiving services.

It is also important for special education directors or supervisors to stay in communication with principals. Principals need to know what expectations have been placed upon the special education teacher, and everyone needs to be on the same page. Often special education teachers receive different expectations from each level of administration because there is not enough communication. It is not educationally beneficial for students when the teacher is expected to do two totally different things with the students.

Support for Professional Development

Special education teachers provide instruction to students, but they also play other roles—that of counselor, nurse, parent, disciplinarian, and behavior specialist, to name a few. They need to have the ability to deal with the diverse needs of each student who receives special education services. Principals need to be flexible and to provide them with the time to attend trainings on a wide range of topics, including:

- Aligning curriculum to the Common Core State Standards
- Safe crisis management
- Positive behavior intervention and supports
- Transition
- Response to intervention
- Universal design for learning
- Direct instruction
- Incorporating technology/assistive technology
- Co-teaching
- Inclusive classroom practices

Even though special education teachers want to be included and involved in inservice training, they also need time to process their piles of paperwork. It is important for principals to keep in mind that special education teachers want to participate in professional development, but do not want their time wasted either. This is a delicate balance and one that requires flexibility. For example, if a school has not met requirements for adequate yearly progress, the principal might arrange for training on differentiated instruction to improve students' assessment scores. Trainings such as these are not as beneficial to special education teachers because they differentiate instruction every day. Another example is when a school is trying to improve students' scores on writing assessments. The training might be geared towards science and social studies content-area teachers, but language arts teachers would not need to be included because they specialize in writing. The rule of thumb here is to carefully evaluate the need for the training and who might benefit most from it.

Effective Inclusion Practices

As discussed in Chapter 5, students with disabilities benefit from being educated in the least restrictive environment (to start, the general education setting)—but only when they receive appropriate support and instruction. Principals need to support special education teachers in regards to requirements for the general education classroom and special education programming. For example, a student whose IEP includes the accommodation of "*opportunities* to test in a smaller environment," general education teachers should not focus on the fact that the IEP does not "require" this, but rather adhere to the intent of the accommodation. Similarly, general education teachers should work with special education staff to ensure that students are adequately prepared for tests and assessments, such as making arrangements for students to receive support (e.g., testing/previewing/reviewing materials). One of a principal's responsibilities is to ensure that general education teachers understand the need for and implement students' accommodations and that they collaborate with special educators to ensure students are fully supported in different education settings.

This support extends to ensuring that general education teachers provide adequate feedback to a student's IEP team or case manager. When a student is not successful in the general education classroom or a content-area class, the student's team or special education teacher needs to know as soon as possible, rather than learning about the situation when it is too late to resolve the issue (e.g., by completing missing assignments, previewing material, or retesting). Therefore, another responsibility for the principal is to ensure that general education teachers communicate frequently with the special education teachers. Note that this is a reciprocal process: When special education teachers are aware of upcoming assignments, tests, and other classroom activities, they can preview information and provide students (as needed) with a better foundation of knowledge that will enhance the general education teacher's instruction on those concepts.

General education teachers are often quick to come to the special education teacher prior to trying any type of intervention or behavior modification. Principals can facilitate this relationship, too: Special educators need to realize there are times when the general education teacher just needs a few ideas to try. Spending time educating general education teachers about the principles of positive behavioral supports and interventions (see Chapter 7) will help them look at student management and discipline challenges with a new eye (i.e., what is the antecedent to the behavior? What is the student trying to achieve or obtain by behaving this way?). This knowledge helps determine what strategy or intervention should be put into place. Having both general education and special education teacher track problem behaviors using a chart or graph of some kind will help determine if the intervention is working. After collecting data over a period of time (e.g., 3–4 weeks), the teachers can together analyze the data to establish whether the intervention is working, or if it needs to be adapted (see box, "A Word About Behavior").

A Word About Behavior

Principals need to be supportive when teachers need to collaborate regarding a student's behavior and the challenges it presents in the general education setting. A group of teachers may need to meet to determine if the behavior is happening in more than one class; something else to bear in mind is that students can have more than one trigger that sets their problem behaviors into motion. For example, a behavior might occur because students are bored or confused, do not like the person assigned to sit beside them, have something that they are upset over, and so on. Students may not feel comfortable asking for help no matter what has happened and need time to talk to someone they trust and feel comfortable being around. The person the student may feel the most comfortable talking to might even be the principal. Not only do special education teachers, general education teachers, and many other staff members need the support of the principal, but students—special education or general education students—also need the principal to be there when needed. When dealing with student discipline, special education teachers expect principals to support them.

Although special education teachers often have smaller class sizes or caseloads, they are still in need of a great amount of support from a variety of people, including general education teachers. To ensure special educators receive the support they need from general education teachers, principals must fully support the planning, programming, and implementation of special education services.

Working With Families

Principals play many different roles in the field of education. As discussed in previous chapters, principals should be prepared to step into the role of local education agency representative on IEP teams—and not just for 5 minutes in order to make an appearance (see Chapter 4). By fully participating in the IEP meeting, the principal demonstrates support both of the special education staff in the building and of the special education process. This is extremely beneficial for the entire team (i.e., students, families, teachers, and the school district). This is also a best practice for limiting or avoiding litigation.

At IEP meetings when there are disagreements or difficulty resolving issues with a student's parent or guardian, the special education teacher needs the steadfast support of the principal. When attending, the principal needs to be prepared to participate and to fully support the special education teacher, general education teachers, and any related service providers. The principal also needs to have enough familiarity with the situation, however, to be able to judge if the meeting should be suspended and rescheduled for another day, while respecting the professional positions of the staff. In addition, principals need to understand the different support needs of the veteran teacher and the first-year or novice special educator.

Quick Review

If not properly cared for, a paper cut can become sore, bothersome, and can take a long time to heal. No matter how creative or great a teacher is or how well the lesson is planned, the learning process may be more difficult if it takes place at all for students with that figurative paper cut. A principal who provides a supportive system will assist in the healing process and enable all students to engage in learning.

References

ADA Amendments Act of 2008, Pub. L. No. 110-325, 122 Stat. 3553, to be codified at 42 U.S.C. § 12101 (2009).

Alwell, M., & Cobb, B. (2009). Social and communicative interventions and transition outcomes for youth with disabilities. *Career Development for Exceptional Individuals, 32*, 94–107. http://dx.doi.org/10.1177/0885728809336657

American School Counselor Association. (2010a). *ASCA National Model: A framework for school counseling programs* (3rd ed.). Alexandria, VA: Author.

American School Counselor Association. (2010b). *Ethical standards for school counselors*. Retrieved from http://www.schoolcounselor.org/asca/media/asca/home/EthicalStandards2010.pdf

American School Counselor Association. (n.d.). *ASCA National Model: Delivery system*. Retrieved from http://www.ascanationalmodel.org/delivery-system

Americans With Disabilities Act of 1990 (ADA, Pub. L. No. 101-336, 1990).

Beck, A. T. (1996). *Beck depression inventory*. San Antonio, TX: Pearson Clinical Psychology.

Brown v. Board of Education, 347 U.S. 483 (1954).

Canter, A. (2003, November). Psychological evaluations: What every principal should know. *Principal Leadership, 4*(3). Retrieved from http://www.naspcenter.org/principals/nassp_evaluation.html

Cedar Rapids Community School District v. Garret F., 526 U.S. 66 (1999).

Chandler, L. K., & Dahlquist, C. M. (2010). *Functional assessment: Strategies to prevent and remediate challenging behavior in school settings* (3rd ed.). Upper Saddle River, NJ: Merrill Prentice Hall.

City, E. A., Elmore, R. F., Fiarman, S. E., & Teitel, L. (2009). *Instructional rounds in education*. Cambridge, MA: Harvard Education Press.

Conley, D. (2007). *Toward a more comprehensive conception of college readiness*. Eugene, OR: Educational Policy Improvement Center. Retrieved from http://www.metrolibraries.net/pro/pdfs/CollegeReadinessPaper.pdf

Conners, C. K. (2008). *Conners 3rd edition*. North Tonawanda, NY: Multi-Health Systems.

Council for Exceptional Children. (1998). *Retention of special education professionals: A practical guide of strategies and activities for educators and administrators*. Retrieved from http://www.personnelcenter.org/pdf/retguide.pdf

Council for Exceptional Children. (2009a). *CEC's policy on restraint and seclusion procedures in school settings*. Retrieved from https://www.cec.sped.org/~/media/Files/Policy/CEC%20Professional%20Policies%20and%20Positions/restraint%20and%20seclusion.pdf

Council for Exceptional Children. (2009b). *What every special educator must know: Ethics, standards, and guidelines*. (6th edition). Arlington, VA: Author.

Council for Exceptional Children. (2010). *CEC policy manual*. Retrieved from http://www.cec.sped.org/~/media/Files/Policy/CEC%20Professional%20Policies%20and%20Positions/policy%20manual.pdf

Council for Exceptional Children. (2012). *The Council for Exceptional Children's position on special education teacher evaluation*. Arlington, VA: Author. Retrieved from https://www.cec.sped.org/~/media/Files/Policy/CEC%20Professional%20Policies%20and%20Positions/Position_on_Special_Education_Teacher_Evaluation_Background.pdf

Daniel R. R. v. State Bd. of Educ., 874 F.2d 1036 (5th Cir. 1989).

Dunlap, G., Iovannone, R., Kincaid, D., Wilson, K., Christiansen, K., Strain, P., & English, C. (2010). *Prevent–teach–reinforce: The school-based model of individualized positive behavior support*. Baltimore, MD: Paul H. Brookes.

Dunlap, G., Kern-L., DePerczel, M., Clarke, S., Wilson, D., Childs, K. E., … Falk, G. D. (1993). Functional analysis of classroom variables for students with emotional and behavioral disorders. *Behavioral Disorders, 18*, 275–291.

Dunn, L. M. (1968). Special education for the mildly retarded: Is much of it justifiable? *Exceptional Children, 23*, 5–21.

Education for All Handicapped Children Act of 1975, Pub. L. No. 94-142, 89 Stat. 773, codified at 20 U.S.C. § 1400

Engelmann, S., Meyer, L., Carnine, L., Becker, W., Eisele, J., & Johnson, G. (1999). *SRA corrective reading: Decoding strategies*. Columbus, OH: SRA/McGraw-Hill.

Fallon, L. M., O'Keeffe, B. V., & Sugai, G. (2012). Consideration of culture and context in school-wide positive behavior support: A review of current literature. *Journal of Positive Behavior Interventions, 14*, 209–219. http://dx.doi.org/10.1177/1098300712442242

Family Educational Rights and Privacy Act of 1974, 20 U.S.C. § 1232g (2006).

Flexer, R. W., Baer, R. M., Luft, P., & Simmons, T. J. (2013). *Transition planning for secondary students with disabilities* (4th ed.). Upper Saddle River, NJ: Pearson.

Frey, N., & Fisher, D. (2013). *Rigorous reading: 5 access points for comprehending complex texts*. Newberry Park, CA: Corwin.

Friend, M. (2007). *Co-teaching approaches*. Retrieved from http://www.marilynfriend. com/approaches.htm

Friend, M., & Bursuck, W. D. (2009). *Including students with special needs: A practical guide for classroom teachers* (5th ed.). Upper Saddle River, NJ: Pearson.

Friend, M., & Cook, L. (2013). *Interactions: Collaboration skills for school professionals* (7th ed.). Upper Saddle River, NJ: Pearson.

Gable, R. A., Quinn, M. M., Rutherford, R. B., Howell, K. W., & Hoffman, C. C. (1998). *Addressing student problem behavior--Part II: Conducting a functional assessment*. Washington, DC: Center for Effective Collaboration and Practice.

Ganser, T. (2002). The new teacher mentors: Four trends that are changing the look of mentoring programs for new teachers. *American School Board Journal, 189*, 25–27.

Geltner, J., & Leibforth, T. (2008). Advocacy in the IEP process: Strengths-based school counseling in action. *Professional School Counseling, 12*, 162–165. http:// dx.doi.org/10.5330/PSC.n.2010-12.162

Gray, C. A., & Garand, J. D. (1993). Social stories: Improving responses of students with autism with accurate social information. *Focus on Autistic Behavior, 8*(1), 1–10.

Grossman, B. G., & Aspy, R. (2011). Comprehensive behavior interventions for individuals with autism spectrum disorders. In E. A. Boutot & B. Smith-Myles, (Eds.), *Autism spectrum disorders: Foundations, characteristics, and effective strategies* (pp. 163–178). Upper Saddle River, NJ: Pearson.

Gruenert, S. (2008, March/April). School culture, school climate: They are not the same thing. *Principal*, 56-59.

Hallahan, D. P., & Kauffman, J. M. (2005). *Special education: What it is and why we need it*. New York, NY: Pearson.

Hanson, A. (2005). Have zero tolerance school discipline policies turned in a nightmare? The American dream's promise of educational opportunity grounded in *Brown v. Board of Education*. *UC Davis Journal of Juvenile Law & Policy, 9*, 289-379. Retrieved from http://jjlp.law.ucdavis.edu/archives/vol-9-no-2/02%20hanson%20final.pdf

Henley, M. (2010). *Classroom management: A proactive approach*. Boston, MA: Pearson.

Holcomb-McCoy, C. (2007). *School counseling to close the achievement gap*. Thousand Oaks, CA: Corwin.

Horner, R. H., & Carr, E. G. (1997). Behavioral support for students with severe disabilities: Functional assessment and comprehensive intervention. *The Journal of Special Education, 31*, 84–104. http://dx.doi.org/10.1177/002246699703100108

House, R. J., Shane, S. A., & Herold, D. M. (1996). Rumors of the death of dispositional research are vastly exaggerated. *Academy of Management Review, 21*, 203–224.

Hoyle, J. R., English, F., & Steffy, B. (1998). *Skills for 21st century school leaders.* Oxford, UK: Rowman & Littlefield Education.

IDEA regulations, 34 C.F.R. § 300 (2012).

Individuals With Disabilities Education Act, 20 U.S.C. §§ 1400 et seq. (2006 & Supp. V. 2011)

Keigher, A., & Cross, F. (2010, August). *Teacher attrition and mobility: Results from the 2008–09 teacher follow-up survey* (NCES 2010-353). Washington, DC: U.S. Department of Education, National Center for Education Statistics.

Madaus, J. W., & Shaw, S. F. (2008). The role of school professionals in implementing Section 504 for students with disabilities. *Journal of Interprofessional Care, 19*, 338–378. http://dx.doi.org/10.1177/0895904807307069

Mastropieri, M. A., & Scruggs, T. E. (2010). *The inclusive classroom: Strategies for effective differentiated instruction.* Upper Saddle River, NJ: Merrill.

Milsom, A., & Dietz, L. (2009). Defining college readiness for students with learning disabilities: A Delphi study. *Professional School Counseling, 12*, 315–323. http://dx.doi.org/10.5330/PSC.n.2010-12.315

National Governors Association Center for Best Practices, Council of Chief State School Officers. (2010). *Common core state standards.* Washington, DC: Author Retrieved from http://www.corestandards.org/

NCLB regulations, 34 C.F.R. § 200 (2012).

No Child Left Behind Act of 2001, 20 U.S.C. §§ 6301 et seq. (2006 & Supp. V. 2011)

Oberti v. Board of Education, 995 F.2d 1204 (3rd Cir. 1993).

Office of Civil Rights. (2009, March). *Protecting students with disabilities: Frequently asked questions about Section 504 and the education of children with disabilities.* Retrieved from https://www2.ed.gov/about/offices/list/ocr/504faq.html

Olsson, C. A., Bond, L., Burns, J. M., Vella-Brodrick, D. A., & Sawyer, S. M. (2003). Adolescent resilience: A concept analysis. *Journal of Adolescence, 26*, 1–11. http://dx.doi.org/10.1016/S0140-1971(02)00118-5

Osgood, R. L. (2005). *The history of inclusion in the United States.* Washington, DC: Gallaudet University Press.

Osher, D., & Boccanfuso, C. (2011, September 20). *Making the case for the importance of school climate and its measurement in turnaround schools* [Webinar]. Retrieved from: http://www.ocde.us/HealthyMinds/Documents/Turnaround%20schools%20and%20school%20climate%20OSher%20USDOE%20OTA%20Making%20the%20Case.pdf

Pennsylvania Department of Education. (2013). *Pennsylvania value added assessment system.* Retrieved from http://www.portal.state.pa.us/portal/server.pt/community/state_assessment_system/20965/pennsylvania_value_added_assessment_system_(pvaas)/1426500

Rehabilitation Act of 1973, as amended by Pub. L. No. 110-325, to be codified at 29 U.S.C. § 701 (2009).

Reinhartz, J., & Beach, D. M. (2004). *Educational leadership: Changing schools, changing roles*. Boston, MA: Pearson Education.

Reynolds, C. R., & Kamphaus, R. W. (2004). BASC-2: *Behavior assessment system for children, second edition manual*. Circle Pines, MN: American Guidance Service.

Reynolds, C. R., Skiba, R. J., Graham, S., Sheras, P., Conoley, J. C., & Garcia-Vazquez, E. (2008). Are zero tolerance policies effective in the schools? An evidentiary review and recommendations. *American Psychologist, 63,* 852–862. http://dx.doi.org/10.1037/0003-066X.63.9.852

Roid, G. H. (2003). *Stanford-Binet intelligence scales (SB5), Fifth edition*. Boston, MA: Houghton Mifflin Harcourt.

Roncker v. Walter, 700 F.2d 1058 (6th Cir., 1983), cert. denied, 464 U.S. 864 (1983).

Rothstein, L. F., & Johnson, S. F. (2013). *Special education law*. Thousand Oaks, CA: SAGE.

Scheuermann, B. K., & Hall, J. A. (2012). *Positive behavioral supports for the classroom*. Upper Saddle River, NJ: Pearson Education.

Schmidt, J. (2014). *Counseling in schools: Comprehensive programs of responsive services for all students* (6th ed.). Upper Saddle River, NJ: Pearson.

Section 504 Regulations, 34 C.F.R. § 100 (2012).

Shapiro, E. (2010). *Academic skills problems* (4th ed.). New York, NY: Guilford.

Skiba, R. J. (2000). *Zero tolerance, zero evidence: An analysis of school disciplinary practice* (Policy Research Report #SRS2). Bloomington: Indiana Education Policy Center.

Skiba, R. J., Albrecht, S. F., & Losen, D. J. (2013). CCBD's position summary on federal policy on disproportionality in special education. *Behavioral Disorders, 38,* 108-120.

Sugai, G., & Simonsen, B. (2012, June). *Positive behavior interventions and supports: History, defining features, and misconceptions*. Storrs: University of Connecticut Center for PBIS and Center for Positive Behavioral Interventions and Supports. Retrieved from http://www.pbis.org/school/pbis_revisited.aspx

Turnbull, A., Turnbull, R., Erwin, E., Soodak, L., & Shogren, K. (2010). *Families, professionals, and exceptionality*. Upper Saddle River, NJ, and Columbus, OH: Pearson.

U.S. Department of Education. (1980). *To assure the free appropriate public education of all handicapped children. Second annual report to Congress on the Education for the Handicapped Act*. Washington, DC: Author.

U.S. Department of Education. (1988). *To assure the free appropriate public education of all handicapped children. Tenth annual report to Congress on the Education for the Handicapped Act*. Washington, DC: Author.

U.S. Department of Education, Office of Special Education and Rehabilitative Services. (2011, December). *30th annual report to Congress on the implementation of the Individuals With Disabilities Education Act, 2008*. Washington, DC: Author. Retrieved from http://www2.ed.gov/about/reports/annual/osep/2008/parts-b-c/30th-idea-arc.pdf

U.S. Department of Education, Office of Special Education Programs. (2013). *SPeNSE fact sheet: Study of personnel needs in special education*. Retrieved from http://education.ufl.edu/spense/files/2013/05/Paperwork.pdf

U.S. Department of Education, OSEP Technical Assistance Center on Positive Behavior Interventions & Supports. (2013). *School-wide PBIS*. Retrieved from http://www.pbis.org/school/default.aspx

Vincent, C. G., Randall, C., Cartledge, G., Tobin, T. J., & Swain-Bradway, J. (2011). Toward a conceptual integration of cultural responsiveness and schoolwide positive behavior support. *Journal of Positive Behavior Interventions, 13*, 219–229. http://dx.doi.org/10.1177/1098300711399765

Warger, C. (1999, September). *Positive behavior support and functional assessment*. Arlington, VA: ERIC Clearinghouse on Disabilities and Gifted Education. Retrieved from http://ericec.org/digests/e580.html

Wechsler, D. (2004). *The Wechsler intelligence scale for children—Fourth edition*. London, England: Pearson Assessment.

Wheeler, J., & Richey, D. (2014). *Behavior management: Principles and practices of positive behavior support*. Boston, MA: Pearson.

Woodcock, R. W., Mather, N., & McGrew, K. S. (2001). *Woodcock–Johnson III tests of cognitive abilities examiner's manual*. Itasca, IL: Riverside.

Appendix A
Internet Resources

Special education law and regulations	
U.S. Supreme Court	http://www.supremecourt.gov/
	Supreme Court of the United States blog (http://www.scotusblog.com/)
	Supreme Court Tracking Chart (http://www.nsba.org/SchoolLaw/SupremeCourt/Relevant-Cases/TrackingChart.pdf)
U.S. Department of Education Office for Civil Rights	http://www2.ed.gov/ocr
U.S. Department of Education Office of Special Education Programs	http://www2.ed.gov/about/offices/list/osers/osep/
Individuals With Disabilities Education Act	http://idea.ed.gov/
	https://www.ideadata.org/default.asp
	http://www.ideapartnership.org/
Section 504 of the Rehabilitation Act	http://www2.ed.gov/about/offices/list/ocr/504faq.html
	National Center for Learning Disabilities' "Section 504 and IDEA Comparison Chart": http://www.ncld.org/disability-advocacy/learn-ld-laws/adaaa-section-504/section-504-idea-comparison-chart
Section 508 of the Rehabilitation Act	http://www2.ed.gov/policy/gen/guid/assistivetech.html
	The Center on Online Learning and Students with Disabilities focuses on the access, participation, and progress of students with disabilities and online learning environments.
	National Association of State Directors of Special Education (http://www.nasdse.org/Projects/CenteronOnlineLearningSWDs/ tabid/420/Default.aspx)
	Center on Online Learning and Students with Disabilities (http://centerononlinelearning.org/)
Americans With Disabilities Act	http://www2.ed.gov/about/offices/list/ocr/docs/hq9805.html
General resources	Wrights Law (http://www.wrightslaw.com/)
	National School Boards Association Legal Clips (http://legalclips.nsba.org/)

Special education news and resources	
American Association on Intellectual and Developmental Disabilities (AAIDD)	http://aaidd.org/
Association for the Gifted (TAG)	http://www.cectag.org/
Council for Children With Behavioral Disorders (CCBD)	http://www.ccbd.net/
Council for Exceptional Children (CEC)	http://www.cec.sped.org/
CEC SmartBrief	https://www.smartbrief.com/ signupSystem/subscribe.action? pageSequence=1&briefName=cec
Council for Educational Diagnostic Services (CEDS)	http://community.cec.sped.org/CEDS/
Council of Administrators of Special Education (CASE)	http://www.casecec.org/
Division for Culturally and Linguistically Diverse Exceptional Learners (DDEL)	http://community.cec.sped.org/DDEL/
Division for Learning Disabilities (DLD)	http://teachingld.org/
Division for Physical, Health and Multiple Disabilities (DPHMD)	http://community.cec.sped.org/DPHMD/
Division on Autism and Developmental Disabilities (DADD)	http://daddcec.org/
Division on Career Development and Transition (DCDT)	http://www.dcdt.org/
Division on Visual Impairments (DVI)	http://community.cec.sped.org/DVI/
Education Week	http://www.edweek.org/topics/ specialeducation/
LDOnline	http://www.ldonline.org/
National Center for Learning Disabilities	http://www.ncld.org/
National Center for Special Education Research (NCSER)	http://ies.ed.gov/ncser/
National Center on Secondary Education and Transition (NCSET)	http://www.ncset.org/
National Institute on Disability and Rehabilitation Research (NIDRR)	http://www2.ed.gov/about/offices/list/ osers/nidrr/
OSEP Ideas That Work: Tool Kit on Teaching and Assessing Students With Disabilities	http://www.osepideasthatwork.org/ toolkit/index.asp
PACER Center	http://www.pacer.org/
TEACCH Autism Program	http://teacch.com/

Topics in instructional leadership	
Principal leadership and development	The Wallace Foundation provides research-based articles, videos, and research reports on school leadership; see http://www.wallacefoundation.org/
	Leadership Matters: What the Research Says About the Importance of Principal Leadership (National Association of Secondary School Principals and National Association of Elementary School Principals, 2013) http://www.naesp.org/sites/default/files/ LeadershipMatters.pdf
	The AWSP Leadership Framework to Support Principal Development (Association of Washington School Principals, 2013) http://tpep-wa.org/wp-content/uploads/AWSP_ Framework_Version_2.0.pdf
	What It Takes to Be an Instructional Leader (Jenkins, 2009) http://www.naesp.org/resources/2/Principal/2009/J-F_ p34.pdf
Instructional core	*The (Only) Three Ways to Improve Performance in Schools* [video with Richard Elmore] http://www.uknow.gse.harvard.edu/leadership/ leadership001a.html
	In Conversation: Leading the Instructional Core. An Interview With Richard Elmore (Constante, 2010) http://www.edu.gov.on.ca/eng/policyfunding/ leadership/summer2010.pdf
	Focus on the Instructional Core (National Staff Development Council, 2009) http://learningforward.org/docs/the-learning-principal/ lp12-08roy.pdf?sfvrsn=2
	From Policy to Reality – What Will Prepare Our Students for Success? [video presentation by Richard Elmore] http://www.youtube.com/watch?v=YXBwt1P2iD4

Topics in instructional leadership	
Co-teaching	Marilyn Friend's Co-Teaching Connection
	http://www.marilynfriend.com
	Pennsylvania Training and Technical Assistance Network's co-teaching resources (PowerPoints, articles, and learning modules)
	http://www.iu17.org/best-practices/resources-modules/co-teaching/
	Co-teaching handouts (definitions, models, and planning tools)
	http://www3.bucksiu.org/cms/lib3/PA09000729/ Centricity/Domain/64/ AllHandouts%20Coteaching.pdf
	6 Steps to Successful Co-Teaching: Helping Special and Regular Education Teachers Work Together (Marston, n.d.)
	http://www.nea.org/tools/6-steps-to-successful-co-teaching.html
	50 Ways to Keep Your Co-Teacher: Strategies for Before, During, and After Co-Teaching (Murawski & Dieker, 2008)
	http://www.2teachllc.com/50%20ways_TEC.pdf
	5 Keys to Co-Teaching in Inclusive Classrooms (Murawski, 2008)
	http://www.aasa.org/SchoolAdministratorArticle.aspx?id=4906
Evidence-based practices	What Works Clearinghouse: http://ies.ed.gov/ncee/wwc/
Discipline	The U.S. Department of Education maintains a web page with extensive information pertaining to disciplinary actions and students with disabilities, including text, videos, and the legislation and regulations in their entirety:
	http://idea.ed.gov/explore/view/p/ %2Croot%2Cdynamic %2CTopicalArea%2C6%2C

Topics in instructional leadership	
Positive behavior interventions and supports (PBIS)	CEC webinars on behavior and PBIS include information on functional behavior assessments, bullying prevention and intervention, schoolwide supports, and developing individual student positive behavior support plans; visit http://www.cec.sped.org/Professional-Development/Webinars/Recorded-Webinars
	U.S. Department of Education Office of Special Education Programs, Technical Assistance Center on PBIS: http://www.pbis.org/
	PBIS World has a list of behaviors that users can select, which are linked to tiered interventions. The site also has information on assessment and data tracking. http://www.pbisworld.com/
	Positive Action behavior education program: https://www.positiveaction.net/
	Deescalation training and crisis management:
	Right Response (http://rightresponse.org/)
	Satori Alternatives to Managing Aggression (http://samatraining.com/)
	Professional Crisis Management Association (http://www.pcma.com/)
Functional behavior assessments (FBA) and behavior intervention plans (BIP)	Resources on FBAs: http://cecp.air.org/fba/ http://www.behavioradvisor.com/FBA.html http://nichcy.org/schoolage/behavior/behavassess http://iris.peabody.vanderbilt.edu/fba/chalcycle.htm http://dese.mo.gov/se/ep/documents/LewisPP.pdf http://www.ideapartnership.org/documents/ASD-Collection/asd-dg_Brief_FBA.pdf
	Resources on BIPs: http://www.behaviorinterventionplan.org/ http://www.pbisworld.com/tier-2/behavior-intervention-plan-bip/

Topics in instructional leadership	
Restraint and seclusion	See CEC policies and information at
	http://www.cec.sped.org/Policy-and-Advocacy/More-Issues/Restraint-and-Seclusion?sc_lang=en
Cultural responsiveness	National Center for Culturally Responsive Educational Systems: www.nccrest.org
	National Center for Cultural Competence: http://nccc.georgetown.edu/
Special education teacher evaluation	See CEC policy, initiatives, and resources at https://www.cec.sped.org/Policy-and-Advocacy/More-Issues/Special-Education-Teacher-Evaluation?sc_lang=en

Appendix B
Federal Definitions

Term	Federal Definition
Child with a disability	A child with intellectual disabilities, hearing impairments (including deafness), speech or language impairments, visual impairments (including blindness), serious emotional disturbance (referred to in this chapter as "emotional disturbance"), orthopedic impairments, autism, traumatic brain injury, other health impairments, or specific learning disabilities; and who, by reason thereof, needs special education and related services.
	This includes children with developmental delays: a child with a developmental delay (age 3-9) is one who is experiencing developmental delays, as defined by the State and as measured by appropriate diagnostic instruments and procedures, in one or more of the following areas: Physical development, cognitive development, communication development, social or emotional development, or adaptive development; and who, by reason thereof, needs special education and related services
Autism	A developmental disability significantly affecting verbal and nonverbal communication and social interaction, generally evident before age three, that adversely affects a child's educational performance. Other characteristics often associated with autism are engagement in repetitive activities and stereotyped movements, resistance to environmental change or change in daily routines, and unusual responses to sensory experiences.
	Autism does not apply if a child's educational performance is adversely affected primarily because the child has an emotional disturbance.

Term	Federal Definition
Deaf-blindness	Concomitant hearing and visual impairments, the combination of which causes such severe communication and other developmental and educational needs that they cannot be accommodated in special education programs solely for children with deafness or children with blindness.
Deafness	A hearing impairment that is so severe that the child is impaired in processing linguistic information through hearing, with or without amplification that adversely affects a child's educational performance.
Emotional disturbance	A condition exhibiting one or more of the following characteristics over a long period of time and to a marked degree that adversely affects a child's educational performance: • An inability to learn that cannot be explained by intellectual, sensory, or health factors. • An inability to build or maintain satisfactory interpersonal relationships with peers and teachers. • Inappropriate types of behavior or feelings under normal circumstances. • A general pervasive mood of unhappiness or depression. • A tendency to develop physical symptoms or fears associated with personal or school problems. Emotional disturbance includes schizophrenia. The term does not apply to children who are socially maladjusted, unless it is determined that they have an emotional disturbance
Hearing impairment	An impairment in hearing, whether permanent or fluctuating, that adversely affects a child's educational performance but that is not included under the definition of deafness in this section.
Intellectual disability	Significantly subaverage general intellectual functioning, existing concurrently with deficits in adaptive behavior and manifested during the developmental period, that adversely affects a child's educational performance.

Term	Federal Definition
Multiple disabilities	Concomitant impairments (such as intellectual disability-blindness or intellectual disability-orthopedic impairment), the combination of which causes such severe educational needs that they cannot be accommodated in special education programs solely for one of the impairments. Multiple disabilities does not include deaf-blindness.
Orthopedic impairment	Having limited strength, vitality, or alertness, including a heightened alertness to environmental stimuli, that results in limited alertness with respect to the educational environment, that is due to chronic or acute health problems such as asthma, attention deficit disorder or attention deficit hyperactivity disorder, diabetes, epilepsy, a heart condition, hemophilia, lead poisoning, leukemia, nephritis, rheumatic fever, sickle cell anemia, and Tourette syndrome; and adversely affects a child's educational performance.
Specific learning disability	A disorder in one or more of the basic psychological processes involved in understanding or in using language, spoken or written, which disorder may manifest itself in the imperfect ability to listen, think, speak, read, write, spell, or do mathematical calculations. Includes perceptual disabilities, brain injury, minimal brain dysfunction, dyslexia, and developmental aphasia. Does not include a learning problem that is primarily the result of visual, hearing, or motor disabilities, of intellectual disability, of emotional disturbance, or of environmental, cultural, or economic disadvantage.
Speech or language impairment	A communication disorder, such as stuttering, impaired articulation, a language impairment, or a voice impairment, that adversely affects a child's educational performance.

Term	Federal Definition
Traumatic brain injury	An acquired injury to the brain caused by an external physical force, resulting in total or partial functional disability or psychosocial impairment, or both, that adversely affects a child's educational performance. Traumatic brain injury applies to open or closed head injuries resulting in impairments in one or more areas, such as cognition; language; memory; attention; reasoning; abstract thinking; judgment; problem-solving; sensory, perceptual, and motor abilities; psychosocial behavior; physical functions; information processing; and speech. Traumatic brain injury does not apply to brain injuries that are congenital or degenerative, or to brain injuries induced by birth trauma.
Visual impairment	An impairment in vision that, even with correction, adversely affects a child's educational performance. The term includes both partial sight and blindness.

Authority: 34 U.S.C. § 300.

Appendix C
Common Acronyms
in Special Education

504	Section 504 Plan
AA-AAS	Alternate assessments based on alternate achievement standards
AA-MAS	Alternate assessments based on modified achievement standards
AAE	Augmentative and alternative communication
ABA	Applied behavioral analysis
ADA	Americans With Disabilities Act
ADD/ADHD	Attention deficit disorder/attention deficit hyperactivity disorder
APE	Adaptive physical education
ARC	Association for Retarded Citizens (formerly, now simply the Arc)
ASD	Autism spectrum disorder(s)
AT	Assistive technology
AYP	Adequate yearly progress
BD	Behavioral disorder
BIP	Behavior intervention plan
CAPD	Central auditory processing disorder
CBA	Curriculum-based assessment
CFR	Code of Federal Regulations
CP	Cerebral palsy
CST	Child study team/teacher
DD	Developmental disability/disabilities or developmental delay
DSM-V	*Diagnostic and Statistical Manual of Mental Disorders* – 5th edition
EBD	Emotional/behavioral disorder
EBP	Evidence-based practice
ECE	Early childhood education
ESEA	Elementary and Secondary Education Act of 1965
ELL	English language learner
ESE	Exceptional student education
ESL	English as a second language
ESOL	English for speakers of other languages
ESY	Extended school year

FAPE	Free and appropriate public education
FAS	Fetal alcohol syndrome
FASD	Fetal alcohol spectrum disorder(s)
FBA	Functional behavioral assessment
FERPA	Family Educational Rights and Privacy Act
GAD	Generalized anxiety disorder
GT	Gifted and talented
HI	Hearing impaired
ID	Intellectual disability (formerly mental retardation, MR)
IDEA	Individuals with Disabilities Education Act
IEE	Independent educational evaluation
IEP	Individualized education program
IFSP	Individualized family service plan
IQ	Intelligence quotient
LD	Learning disability
LEA	Local education agency
LEP	Limited English proficiency
LRE	Least restrictive environment
MDE	Multidisciplinary evaluation
MDT	Multidisciplinary team
MS	Multiple sclerosis
NCLB	No Child Left Behind Act of 2001
NF	Neurofibromatosis
NLD/NVLD	Nonverbal learning disabilities
OCD	Obsessive compulsive disorder
ODD	Oppositional defiant disorder
OHI	Other health impairment
OSERS	Office of Special Education and Rehabilitative Services
OT	Occupational therapy
OVR	Office of vocational rehabilitation
PBIS	Positive behavior interventions and supports
PDD	Pervasive developmental disorder
PDD-NOS	Pervasive developmental disorder—not otherwise specified
PECS	Picture exchange communication system
PLEP/PLOP	Present levels of educational performance

PT	Physical therapy
RAD	Reactive attachment disorder
RTI	Response to intervention
SI	Sensory integration
SID	Sensory integration dysfunction/disorder
S/L	Speech and language
SLD	Specific learning disability
SPD	Semantic pragmatic disorder
SSI	Supplemental Security Income
TBI	Traumatic brain injury
VI	Visual impairment
VMI	Visual motor integration
VOCA	Voice output communication aids
Tests and measurements	
ABLLS-R	Assessment of Basic Language and Learning Skills, Revised (Partington, 2006)
ABS-S:2	Adaptive Behavior Scale-School, 2nd edition (Lambert, Nihira, & Leland, 1993)
BASC-2	Behavior Assessment System for Children, 2nd edition (Reynolds & Kamphaus, 2004)
Beery VMI	Beery-Buktenica Developmental Test of Visual-Motor Integration, 6th Edition
CAS	Das-Naglieri Cognitive Assessment System (Naglieri & Das, 1997)
CASL	Comprehensive Assessment of Spoken Language (Carrow-Woolfolk, 1999)
CEFL-4	Clinical Evaluation of Language Fundamentals, 4th edition (Semel, Wiig, & Secord, 2003)
CMS	Children's Memory Scale (Cohen, 1997)
COWAT	Controlled Oral Word Association Test (Benton, Hamsher, & Sivan, 1994)
C-TOPP-2	Comprehensive Test of Phonological Processing, 2nd edition (Wagner, Torgesen, Rashotte, & Pearson, 2013)
DAR-2	Diagnostic Assessment of Reading, 2nd edition (Roswell, Chall, Curtis, & Kearns, 2005)
DAS-II	Differential Ability Scales-II (Elliott, 2007)

Tests and measurements	
DIBELS	Dynamic Indicators of Basic Early Literacy Skills, 6th edition (Good & Kaminski, 2002)
DTVP-3	Developmental Test of Visual Perception, 3rd edition (Hammill, Pearson, & Voress, 2013)
GADS	Gilliam Asperger's Disorder Scale (Gilliam, 2000)
GRS	Gifted Rating Scales (Pfeiffer & Jarosewich, 2003)
IRI	Informal Reading Inventory, 8th edition (Roe & Burns, 2010)
ITBS	Iowa Test of Basic Skills (Hoover, Dunbar, & Frisbie, 2001/2007)
KABC-II	Kaufman Assessment Battery for Children, 2nd edition (Kaufman & Kaufman, 2004)
KTEA-II	Kaufman Test of Educational Achievement, 2nd edition (Kaufman & Kaufman, 2004)
NEPSY-II	A Developmental NEuroPSYchological Assessment (Korkman, Kirk, & Kemp, 2007)
NNAT2	Naglieri Nonverbal Ability Test, 2nd edition (Naglieri, Brulles, & Landsdowne, 2008)
PAL-II	Process Assessment of the Learner, 2nd edition (Berninger, 2007)
PASAT	Paced Auditory Serial Addition Test (Gronwell & Sampson, 1974)
QRI-5	Qualitative Reading Inventory, 5th edition (Leslie & Caldwell, 2010)
RPM	Raven's Progressive Matrices (Raven, Raven, & Court, 2004)
SETT	Student, Environment, Tasks, and Tools Framework (Zabala, 2002)
SIB-R	Scales of Independent Behavior-Revised (Bruininks, Woodcock, Weatherman, & Hill, 1996)
SIPT	Sensory Integration and Praxis Test (Ayres, 1989)
TAPS-3	Test of Auditory-Perceptual Skills-3rd edition (Martin & Brownell, 2005)
TEWL-2	Test of Early Written Language-2nd edition (Hresko, Herron, & Peak, 1996)

Tests and measurements	
TLC-E	Test of Language Competence-Expanded Edition (Wiig & Secord, 1989)
TOMAL-2	Test of Memory and Learning, 2nd edition (Reynolds & Vorass, 2007)
TONI-4	Test of Nonverbal Intelligence, 4th edition (Brown, Sherbenou, & Johnsen, 2010)
TOPS-E	Test of Problem Solving-Elementary, Revised (Bowers, Huisingh, Barrett, Orman, & LoGiudice, 1994)
TOWE	Test of Written Expression (McGhee, Bryant, Larsen, & Rivera, 1995)
TOWL-4	Test of Written Language-4th edition (Hammill & Larsen, 2009)
TOWRE-2	Test of Word Reading Efficiency, 2nd edition (Torgesen, Wagner, & Rashotte, 2012)
TVPS-3	Test of Visual-Perceptual Skills, 3rd edition (Martin, 2006)
WAIS-IV	Wechsler Adult Intelligence Scale, Fourth Edition (Wechsler, 2008)
WIAT-III	Wechsler Individual Achievement Test-Third Edition (Wechsler, 2009)
WISC-IV	Wechsler Intelligence Scale for Children-Fourth Edition (Wechsler, 2003)
WMS-IV	Wechsler Memory Scale-Fourth Edition (Wechsler, 2009)
WRAML2	Wide Range Assessment of Memory and Learning, 2nd edition (Sheslow & Adams, 2003)
WRAT4	Wide Range Achievement Test, 4th edition (Wilkinson & Robertson, 2006)

Appendix D
Section 504
Accommodations

This table provides examples of accommodations and services that might be considered for specific disability profiles. As discussed in Chapter 1, students with disabilities that "substantially [limit] one or more major life activities, [including] caring for one's self, performing manual tasks, walking, seeing, hearing, speaking, breathing, learning, working" (34 C.F.R. § 104.3[j][1]–[2][ii]) may be eligible for accommodations under Section 504 of the Rehabilitation Act of 1973.

Disability	Major life activity that is affected	Possible accommodations
ADD/ADHD	Learning—The student is unable to participate in the school's programs to the same degree as students without disabilities and therefore is substantially limited by the disability.	Preferential seating
		Provide concise instructions with concrete steps
		Peer tutors/support
		Direct instruction in compensatory strategies and organizational skills
		Model use of study guides/organizational tools
		Break tests into shorter administrations/provide breaks
		Adapt environment to minimize distractions
		Home–school communication/checklists to monitor progress on assignments
		Grade for content integrity rather than neatness

Disability	Major life activity that is affected	Possible accommodations
Allergies	Breathing—The student's severe allergic reaction may interfere with ability to get to school or participate once there.	Avoid allergy-causing substance (foods; may need air purifier/ventilation) Related services (school clinic aide/nurse/ nutritionist, coaches, laundry service) Accommodate medical appointments Develop health care/ emergency plans including dispensing of medications Adapt physical education curriculum as needed
Arthritis	Performing manual tasks— The student may require a modified physical education program.	Provide rest period during the day Accommodate medical appointments Assistive devices for writing tasks (pencil grips, non-skid surface, computer, note taker, audio recording, outlines or study guides) Adapted PE curriculum Develop health care/ emergency plans including dispensing of medications Seating accommodations Allow extra time between classes/locker assistance Peer support groups/ instructional aide or paraprofessional

Disability	Major life activity that is affected	Possible accommodations
Cancer	Caring for oneself and learning—A student with long-term medical problems may need a class schedule that allows for rest and recuperation.	Adjust attendance policies Home instruction/tutoring Accommodate involvement in extracurricular activities Adapted physical education curriculum Develop health care/emergency plans including dispensing of medications Related services (school clinic aide/nurse, counselor, psychologist) Peer group support/peer tutoring
Cerebral palsy	Walking—The student has serious difficulties with fine and gross motor skills, and uses a wheelchair.	Provide assistive technology devices Allow extra time between classes/provide assistance with carrying books, etc. Adapted physical education curriculum Related services (e.g., physical therapy) Develop health care/emergency plans including dispensing of medications Instructional aide/paraprofessional support Monitor accessibility to classrooms, movement through school hallways/levels

Note. For additional accommodations appropriate for specific disability profiles, see Cambridge Public Schools' "Sample Section 504 Accommodations by Disability," at http://www3.cpsd.us/media/theme/Pro-Cambridge/network/10516/media/CPS%20Redesign/documents/SpecialEducation/Section504/Accommodations_by_Disability.pdf?rev=2

Appendix E
IEP Checklists

Before the IEP meeting	
	Provide parent or guardian with an opportunity to review the student's records.
	Provide parent or guardian with an opportunity to review current evaluations.
	Notify parent or guardian that an independent education evaluation may be obtained when the district's evaluations are inadequate or inappropriate.
	Arrange for the parent or guardian to speak with teacher(s) regarding the student's educational progress in the classroom.
Timetable and requirements for IEP development	
	The IEP meeting is held and the IEP developed within 30 days of the initial determination that the student is eligible for special education and related services.
	The IEP is reviewed at least once a year.
	The parent or guardian is notified of the meeting in sufficient time to arrange attendance.
	The written notice of the meeting includes: ☐ Purpose of the meeting ☐ Time of the meeting ☐ Location of the meeting ☐ Participants in the meeting ☐ Parent/guardian right to invite additional attendees
	The IEP meeting includes all necessary participants: ☐ A representative of the school qualified to provide or supervise special education services ☐ General education teacher(s) ☐ Parent or guardian ☐ The student, as appropriate (age 16+) ☐ A member of the multidisciplinary evaluation team ☐ Others at the parent's or school's discretion ☐ Interpreter, as necessary
	The IEP is in effect at the beginning of the school year.
	Parent/guardian receives a copy of the IEP.

	Content of the IEP
	IEP is developed at the IEP meeting by participants.
	IEP is developed prior to making placement decisions.
	The IEP covers all areas where the student needs specially designed instruction (e.g., academics, communication, socialization, self-help, behavior, fine and gross motor skills).
	The IEP lists the students' present level of educational performance in each area where the student has needs.
	Annual goals, based on the current level of educational performance, state what the student will learn in all areas where the student requires specially designed instruction.
	The IEP includes short-term instructional objectives (i.e., measurable steps developed for each goal) that state what the student will do, under what conditions, and to what criteria.
	The IEP lists any related services the student needs to benefit from special education services (e.g., transportation).
	The IEP lists the beginning date and duration of all specially designed instruction and related services, and the frequency and amount of time spent on each related service.
	The IEP lists the extent of participation in education or school activities with the student's typically developing peers.
	The IEP lists the staff responsible for implementing each area.
	Special considerations — *if any answer is "yes," this needs to be directly addressed in the IEP*
	Is the student blind or visually impaired?
	Is the student deaf or hearing impaired?
	Does the student exhibit behaviors that impede his or her learning or that of others?
	Does the student have limited English proficiency?
	Does the student require assistive technology devices and services?
	Does the student need transition services?
	Will the student be 16 years of age or older within the duration of this IEP?
	Is the student within 3 years of graduation?
	Does the student qualify for extended school year services (ESY)?
	Does the student need adaptive physical education?
	Does the student need any related services?
	Will the student participate in statewide assessments?

Implementation of the IEP	
	The IEP is implemented as soon as possible following the IEP meeting.
	The student's placement is based on the requirements in the IEP.
	The student's placement is as close to home as possible, preferably in the student's neighborhood school.
	The IEP is reviewed and revised as often as needed, but at least once a year.
	The student is reevaluated for special education services every 3 years.
	The parent or guardian is informed of the option to request a due process hearing if unsatisfied with the appropriateness of the educational program specified in the IEP.

Appendix F
Placement Checklist

	Are students' IEPs based on general education standards?
	Do we start by considering the general education classroom with supports and services as the primary option?
	Do we encourage the full participation of students with disabilities in all aspects of school life, including extracurricular activities and events?
	Are non-academic skills taught in "natural" settings, that is, in situations where students would normally need them?
	Are students educated in the least restrictive educational alternative (i.e., in classes with peers without disabilities as much as possible)?
	Is the instructional day for a student with a disability the same length as that of students without disabilities?
	Are the school building and its classrooms physically accessible?
	Do students with disabilities have the same opportunities to participate in extracurricular activities as students without disabilities?
	Are placement decisions made at IEP meetings and not before?
	Are teachers and paraprofessionals trained in current inclusive practices?
	Are staff members willing to collaborate in order to make inclusion work?
	Are all staff members willing to take ownership of students with disabilities?
	Do current practices support inclusive outcomes?
	Have we defined what "success" is for students with disabilities?
	Do teachers understand their role in developing and implementing classroom modifications and accommodations?
	Is our inclusive philosophy aligned with district goals?
	Do we provide all students with a sense of community, and do we help families belong to our school community?

Index

F

G

H

I

P

R

S

Woodcock Johnson Test of Cognitive Abilities, 52
Working With Families, 74

Z

Zero-tolerance, 118